T0308674

Original French edition:
« La guérison des 5 blessures »
First printing: 2015
CAN ISBN 978-2-920932-68-5

© 2017 by Lise Bourbeau
First edition/First printing - April 2017
National library of Canada
Bibliothèque et Archives nationales du Québec
ISBN 978-2-920932-75-3
Printed in Canada

Worldwide print distributor
Lotus Brands Inc.
P.O. Box 325
Twin Lakes, WI
53181 USA
Tel: 262-889-8501 or 1-800-824-6396
Fax: 262-889-2461
Email: **lotuspress@lotuspress.com**
www.lotuspress.com

Publisher
Les Editions E.T.C. Inc.
1102 Boul. La Salette
Saint-Jerome (Quebec)
J5L 2J7 Canada
Tel: 450-431-5336

Email: **info@leseditionsetc.com**
www.leseditionsetc.com

LISE BOURBEAU

BEST-SELLING AUTHOR OF
"Your body's telling you LOVE YOURSELF!"

The only book that shows you why accepting and loving the ego is the only way to heal! and HOW TO go about it.

Ego

Betrayal • Humiliation • Rejection • Abandonment • Injustice

The greatest obstacle to healing the 5 wounds.

Table of contents

Acknowledgments

A big **thank you** to the thousands of readers the world over who shared with me how thrilled they were to discover the five wounds of the soul. The interest you have shown and the stories you shared have encouraged me to write a second book on the topic.

Thank you to all of the *Listen to Your Body* teachers who shared with me the discoveries that they and the participants have made during the numerous workshops they give each year.

Thank you to the thousands of participants who have asked me questions and shared ideas with me, which have encouraged me to improve the teaching of *Listen to Your Body*.

A special **thank you** to my nephew Sylvain who gave me the push I needed by asking me one day when I would be writing about the healing of wounds. I suggested to him and to all of the others who asked me this question to reread the last chapter of my book entitled *Heal your wounds and find your true self*, which deals with this very topic. He replied that he had read it several times but added it was not enough and that he was fed up being overwhelmed by his wounds. Feeling that his request was coming from the depth of his heart and that it was important for him to make progress during his healing process, I decided it would be the theme of my next book.

Thank you David Martin (The Golden Pen Inc., Ottawa) for your professionalism and your excellent translation.

Thank you to Jean-Pierre Gagnon, the General Manager of Éditions ETC, for his great work and constant support.

Thank you to Monica Shields, the CEO of Listen to Your Body and my daughter, for the creation of the book cover, as she has done with most of my other books, since my very first one.

Prologue

Fourteen years have now gone by since I wrote my first book on the five wounds of the soul. I decided the time had come to share with you the numerous discoveries I have made in the time since and to especially emphasize the healing of these wounds which cause suffering to so many people.

Heal your wounds and find your true self [1] continues to break sales records in French-speaking countries and in several foreign countries. By 2014 when I was writing this book, it had been translated into sixteen languages. It dawned on me that devoting just one chapter to the healing of wounds did not seem to be enough, because I was frequently being asked, *"How can we heal our wounds?"*

If you have not read the first book, I strongly suggest you read it, because I cannot repeat all of the information it contains in this second book. In Chapter one, I have prepared a brief overview of the main characteristics to refresh the reader's memory, but I would suggest just the same that you read or reread my first book on that subject. The ego reacts with such terror when confronted by wounds that it does everything in its power to prevent us from understanding or to misinterpret what has been said or written. I will be providing in Chapter three more details on the huge influence of our ego on maintaining wounds.

While reading this book, you may get the impression at times I am not saying exactly the same thing as in the first book. Please do not worry about which version you should believe. The current version is definitely the one to go with, since

[1] Les Editions E.T.C. Inc., 2000

I have discovered many subtleties in the past fourteen years that I was unaware of previously.

With the thousands of workshops that I and my teachers have given over all these years, I can speak much more specifically about wounds on the basis of what we have observed personally and what the participants have noted and shared with us.

In this book, you will learn how to deal with the human dimension that continues to believe that a given behaviour means *rejection*, that another behaviour means *abandonment*, and so on, for the five wounds. Reality is totally different. When you perceive matters from the heart, you have more of an overall perspective and observe both people and situations from a new vantage point.

For example, someone can talk to you in a way that makes you feel rejected, but they are only expressing their needs or limits. As you get to the point that you are just able to observe that you feel a wound, you will discover that these wounds will hurt increasingly less and last for a much shorter period of time.

People have often told me that when they discover their wounds, either by reading the book or attending a workshop, they were angered and even discouraged to learn unpleasant things about themselves. Their first reaction was to deny what they discovered and to put the situation behind them.

It is important that you don't kid yourself into thinking that, going forward, you'll have every "trick in the book" you need to shield yourself from wounds. I am convinced that until such time a person returns to Earth, their wounds prevent them from being themselves, being centered and being in their heart.

The desire to eliminate them is an indication of rejection, not acceptance, just like someone who wants to lose weight rejects himself instead of accepting himself. We know that if we manage to "get rid" of something or someone because we cannot accept it or them, this is but a temporary measure, because the situation returns with a vengeance. It sometimes reappears in a different form, but it causes us just as much suffering.

Recognizing which wound has been activated and how to accept it will help you to avoid using the mask associated with this wound. You will be pleasantly surprised to discover that you can apply balm to the wound very quickly to put an end to your suffering. This balm is called acceptance. The wounds gradually decrease in intensity and hurt increasingly less when they are activated.

I am assuming you're aware of the power of acceptance, as it is a topic that comes back in every one of my books, conferences and all of the workshops. We continue talking about it tirelessly, because the ego remembers past suffering especially and causes us to ignore what we hear that is new.

Please note that any references to the male gender apply equally to women, and if not, specific mention will be made to this effect.

To help you be more aware of the significance of each of your wounds, which is yet another major reason why I wrote this book, I will cite numerous examples of wounds that have been activated. Over the years, I have often asked people very familiar with the topic the following question: *Are you aware of the wound that has been affected in the situation you have just described for me?* And the person would look at me in total surprise, because they only considered their impatience, for example. That is a good example of our ego that prevents us from being aware of each instance where a wound has been activated. How can you heal your injuries gradually when you are not aware that they are causing you to suffer?

Now the only thing left for you to do is open your heart wider to continue your reading. You'll see that a blank page has been provided at the end of every chapter where you can write down what you DECIDE to apply to your life after reading the chapter. I remind you that, in order to experiment with concrete and favourable changes, you must DECIDE to do things differently in your day-to-day lives. You must also accept your not having been able to make changes before.

Two things are infinite: the UNIVERSE and HUMAN STUPIDITY; and I'm not sure about the universe.

Albert Einstein

Chapter One

Reviewing the five wounds

To begin, I remind you that all of us come into the world with wounds we must learn to accept. They have developed over the course of numerous incarnations, and depending on our life plan, some will cause more suffering than others. Suffering is a matter of degree to each of us, and most of us do not know where the suffering comes from or what to do to stop it. All that we know is that many persons and situations cause us to react and therefore suffer. That is why it is so interesting to discover the source of our suffering.

They are called wounds of the soul, because the soul can no longer stand repeatedly being removed from its life plan when we allow our ego to run our life. The soul suffers, because the purpose of its incarnations is to live in true love and self-acceptance to live its divinity.

Our soul suffers differently, depending on the wounds that have been activated. The most unfortunate thing is when we allow our ego to convince us that it is helping us suffer less when, in fact, the opposite is true.

> **It is impossible for the ego to feel the suffering of the soul. It only lives for itself. Its major source of satisfaction is being right.**

The ego's preferred method to avoid having us feel the suffering caused by a wound is to have us wear a mask every time one is activated. It sincerely believes it is protecting us and is unaware of the fact that, by acting this way, all we are doing is maintaining and feeding into our wounds. The more you feed into a wound, the more it hurts. The quicker and stronger our reaction, the longer the reaction lasts.

Why are there so many suicides? Why are there millions of people who become dependent on substances such as cigarettes, sugar, gambling, alcohol, medications and drugs that prevent them from being aware of a real problem? Why are there increasing numbers of serious illnesses, in spite of all the progress science has made? Why are there so many separations and divorces? The reason is because people do not want to feel all the pain their soul is experiencing.

Sadly, if you deny this pain, it only gets worse. You can compare this to a serious physical injury. The wound is open and gradually becomes affected. Even if you try to cover it up so as not to see it, the infection worsens and becomes more painful by the day until you reach your pain threshold. At that point, you've got two choices: you either die from it or take actions to heal it. The human race has now reached this point! It is high time we became aware of how urgent the situation now is, so that we can live the life we all aspire to...a life of happiness, not pain.

After years of observing and listening to people describe many problematic, personal and professional situations, I have realized that we clearly attract behaviours or attitudes from others according to the wounds we have. I have concluded that all of us are affected by at least four of the five wounds. We all suffer from rejection, abandonment, humiliation, betrayal and injustice. The only wound that everyone does not seem to have is humiliation.

Most people admit they have at least two of the four wounds that are more apparent and cause more suffering. On the other hand, if we look back at the changes we have gone through during our life, we can say that some wounds seem to have faded and that others have become more intense.

I personally come from a large family. My parents did the best they could for their eleven children by working hard, but they were not as present and attentive to our needs as we would have liked. They didn't have time to compliment us or listen to us. So why is it that some felt rejected, others abandoned or betrayed, and others suffered more from injustice or humiliation? I know now that what our parents were and did was not the root cause of the suffering associated with our wounds. It was how WE perceived their attitude personally.

> **Our perception or interpretation of the facts is what causes us to suffer, not what someone is or does.**

When discussing wounds in my previous book, I explained that abandonment is hidden behind betrayal and rejection behind injustice, though we don't experience them to the same degree. I suggest that you remember this whenever you feel injustice or betrayal. When trying to find what you are afraid of in a hurtful situation, you will discover that the fears of being rejected and being abandoned are the scariest and cause the most suffering.

I have now come to this certainty, because the two most important and visible wounds on my body have always been betrayal and injustice. For the longest time, I always believed that I had no or very little exposure to abandonment and rejection. Only in the last ten years have I been able to admit that my fears of rejection and abandonment were even more present than the fear of being betrayed or falling victim to injustice.

I remind you as well that the fear of rejecting, abandoning, betraying or being unfair to others is just as important as the fear of what they could do to you. You will also realize that you are hurting yourself to the same degree. You are rejecting yourself, you are abandoning yourself, you are humiliating yourself, you are betraying yourself and you are unfair to yourself to the same degree you are with others, and you suffer just as much. In *Listen to Your Body*, we call this major truth the *Triangle of life*.

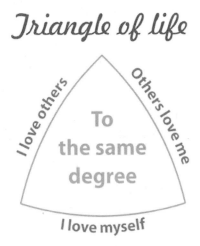

The triangle of life illustrates the fact that others are with you, just as you are with them and with yourself. The degree of suffering – the fears and emotions – is identical.

The following is a summary of the characteristics of each wound and each mask, which you can refer to as you read through the book. Remember that we put on a mask as soon as a wound is activated – either by you or someone else – to protect ourselves.

Our ego tricks us into thinking that we don't have any wounds and is convinced that denial will make it hurt less. **We do all we can to ignore the wound and especially not to feel it, believing also that others will neither see nor feel it.**

The characteristics of each mask differ slightly from those that appeared in my first book, because they include the findings of all of my research and observations since it first appeared.

The wound of rejection

Awakening of the wound: From conception to one year old. The child felt rejected by the parent of the same sex and does not believe in their right to exist.

Mask: withdrawal

Greatest fear: panic

Attitudes and behaviours of the wound when the mask is activated:

— The *withdrawer* firmly believes they're pretty much or even totally worthless. They are constantly dissatisfied with who they are. They consider themselves no good and have very little self-esteem.

— They're convinced that if they didn't exist, it wouldn't make much difference. They think they are different from the rest of their family.

— They feel cut off and misunderstood by others and even by humans in general. They often feel alone, worried and excited in a group.

- They have developed several escape mechanisms (drugs, alcohol, sleep, daydreaming, fleeing situations, virtual games, etc.).

- They unconsciously protect themselves by resorting to denial. They can easily cut themselves off from the outside world by taking refuge in their imaginary world or by daydreaming (astral world). They can even wonder what they are doing on Earth or believe they're in the wrong family.

- They are overcome by emotions, especially by fears, when they are alone.

- They attach little importance to material things: anything relating to the mind or to the intellectual world is more attractive to them.

- They have a very fertile imagination, but unfortunately use it to readily create rejection scenarios.

- They believe, either consciously or not, that happiness is short-lived.

- They generally have little to say and withdraw into a group. They are afraid of bothering others or not being interesting. They are considered loners and are left alone. The more they isolate themselves, the more invisible they seem to become.

- In the presence of someone who raises their voice or becomes aggressive, they quickly extricate themselves from the situation before they panic.

- When people look at them, they immediately worry about what they are.

- They have nervous energy that enables them to take on a huge amount of work. They feel they exist only when they are quite busy, which helps them anchor themselves to the material world.

— They are perfectionists, and as they get older, they become more panicky at the thought they will not be able to cope with life one day.

— They are inclined to believe they've missed their calling in life.

— Their fear of rejection causes them to be obsessive in certain situations.

— They often use the following words: nil, nothing, disappear, non-existent, no room, worthless, etc.

Description of their physique:

— Small, narrow and very slender body.

— Upper body contracted and bent forward.

— Certain parts of the body are smaller.

— A part of the body is missing. (e.g., buttocks, breasts, etc.)

— Body sunken in areas. (chest, back, chest, etc.)

— Some of the body is asymmetrical.

— Small and shifty eyes.

— Mask around the eyes. (deep bags under the eyes)

— Weak and faded voice.

— Skin problems. (especially in the face)

— Likes black clothing.

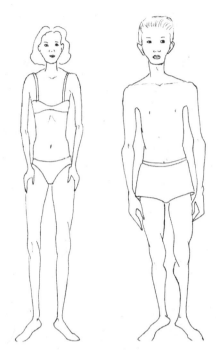

*Body of a person suffering
from the wound of REJECTION
(Mask of Withdrawal)*

Wound of abandonment

Awakening of the wound: between one and three years with the parent of the opposite sex.

A child who has suffered from a lack of support by their parent of the opposite sex in their love-affection connection. They were deprived of affective nourishment or received a form of affection that was not warm or that was different from their expectations.

Mask: Dependence

Greatest fear: Solitude

Attitudes and behaviours of the wound when the mask is activated: The *dependent* person has trouble operating alone and is very fearful of solitude. They seek presence and attention. They especially need support from those around them.

— They often sink into profound sadness, whether alone or not, without really knowing why.

— When they are alone, they can cry for long periods, unaware that they are feeling sorry for themselves.

— They unconsciously cause drama or illnesses to attract pity and attention. They develop a victim's attitude, believing that it is because they are unlucky.

— They bond easily with others, probe the latter's emotions and use their problems to attract attention to themselves.

— They show a star side, which is often dramatic, in the way they express themselves to attract attention. They like to talk about themselves in a group and often turn everything back to themselves.

— They physically latch onto others and have trouble doing or deciding on something alone.

— They often ask others for advice or opinions and can even appear to be unable just to get help, not because they can't perform the task at hand. It is highly likely that they will not even follow the advice going forward, since all they were looking for was attention.

— When they look after or do a favour for someone, their hope is that person will look after them in return.

— They have ups and downs: they're happy one day and unhappy the next. They are easily thrown off by their emotions.

— The difficulty they have ending a relationship causes them to perform many gyrations to avoid ending up alone.

— They believe if someone agrees with them, it's proof of their love.

— When in the presence of someone who is angry or aggressive, they hunker down and act like a small child who is afraid.

— As they get older, they become increasingly anxious about being alone. They choose to put up with a difficult situation rather than be alone.

— They often use words and expressions such as alone, absent, I can't put up with, they don't leave me alone, I let down, etc.

Description of the physical body:

— Long, thin and untoned body.

— Underdeveloped muscle system.

— Arms seem to be too long and dangle alongside the body.

— Sloped shoulders.

— Curved back arching forward.

— Part of the body sagging or flaccid.

— Part of the body lower than normal.

— Large, unhappy or droopy eyes.

— Small, child-like and plaintive voice.

— Likes full or baggy clothes.

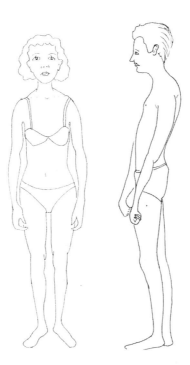

Body of a person suffering from
the wound of ABANDONMENT
(Dependent mask)

Wound of humiliation

Awakening of the wound: between the ages of one and three with the parent that repressed all forms of physical pleasure. This wound could have been experienced with one of the parents – the one who looked after the child's physical and sexual development – or both.

A child who suffered humiliation from a parent for experiencing pleasure with their senses. Their freedom was curtailed by a repressive and vexatious attitude. They suffered shame at the hands of this parent.

Mask: Masochism

Greatest fear: Freedom

Attitudes and behaviours of the wound when the mask is activated: The *masochist* has a fine missionary soul but often manifests it out of fear.

— They seem to believe that God (or the family's moral guardian) is observing and judging them incessantly. They do everything they can to be worthy in the eyes of God or those they love. They believe they must relieve the suffering of humanity to be spiritual and worthy. That is why they make it their duty to serve everyone they love and put these people before themselves. On the other hand, a *masochist* has difficulty being mothered.

— They are very guarded in what they say, having learned they are not supposed to say things that could harm others especially. They are even inclined to find excuses for others.

— They do not want to get in touch with their sensuality and their love of pleasure associated with the senses.

— They repress urges associated with their senses, because they fear going overboard and being ashamed.

— They also fear being punished if they get too much enjoyment out of life.

— There are often stories with a sexual component dating back to their childhood and their adolescence.

— They see to it they are not free, because "being free" to them means "not having boundaries and overindulging in pleasure."

— They therefore curtail their freedom by putting others' needs before their own, depriving them of time to enjoy life. They believe that enjoying their senses takes them away from their spirituality. In addition, they do not want to be labelled heartless.

— They know their needs but don't listen to them, believing they must sacrifice themselves to deserve going to Heaven when they die.

— They can easily feel unclean, dirty or indignant. They sometimes even disgust themselves.

— They compensate and often reward themselves with food, wanting to believe they are enjoying it, but the guilt and shame they feel negate any enjoyment.

— They readily put on weight to give themselves a reason not to enjoy their senses.

— They have a knack of making other people laugh by deriding themselves, thereby inflicting humiliation on themselves.

— They are attracted by or only allow themselves small things, because they do not see their generosity of spirit.

— They often use the following words: worthy, unworthy, small, large, I'm stuck, pig, messy, dirty, etc.

Description description of the physical body

— Overweight, but round instead of large.

— Short in stature.

— Round, open face.

— Round eyes that are open and reflect the naivety of a child.

— Large neck.

— Buffalo hump in the upper back.

— Part of the body round or roundish.

— Often wears tight clothes, which accentuates the roundness.

— Frequently stains their clothing.

— Smooth voice.

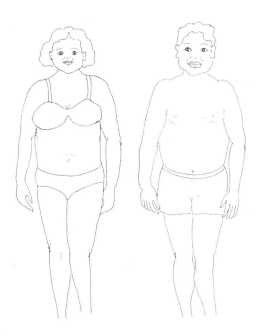

*Body of a person suffering
from the wound of
HUMILIATION (Masochist*

Wound of betrayal

Awakening of the wound: between two and four years of age with the parent of the opposite sex.

A disappointed child who has suffered from not having been given the attention they felt they deserved from the parent of the opposite sex. They felt betrayed or manipulated in their love-sexuality connection. They lost confidence in this parent, having witnessed unkept promises, lies or signs of weakness. They determined that the parent did not shoulder their responsibilities.

Mask: Control

Greatest fear: Dissociation, separation and disavowal

Attitudes and behaviours of the wound when the mask is activated: The *controller* goes to great lengths to convince others of their strong personality. They use their qualities as leader to impose their will.

— They are detached from their vulnerability and seek to pass themselves off as strong. They make it a point to have others know what they are capable of.

— They perform in a way that they are considered very responsible. They believe that by being responsible, they are a leader. In actual fact, they are irresponsible, because they accuse and shift the blame to others. They easily come up with ways to avoid having fingers pointed at them.

— They seek to be special and important. They pursue honours and designations, thereby capturing a lot of attention in a group setting.

— They are easily impressed by the presence of a wealthy or famous person and trusts them readily. They let their guard down, and if they are disappointed, they end up being distrustful.

— Their reputation is very important to them. If they feel it is threatened, they are willing to tarnish someone else's.

— They lie easily to get out of a tight spot. However, they can't stand it when someone else lies. The lie is what bothers them, not the action. For example, if a man cheats on his wife, she will be more upset by the lie than his having met someone else.

— They have a lot of expectations of others and are demanding. When they delegate, they demand that it be done both
in the manner and at the pace they like in order to feel
superior and important. Their lack of trust prompts them
to check incessantly.

— They like to anticipate everything to have better control.
They cannot stand having someone come along and disrupt
their plans. They have trouble accepting contingencies.

— They believe they are indispensable and like to think that
others would not succeed without them.

— They have a difficult time opening up and admitting things
readily, as they do not trust members of the opposite sex.
They fear being taken advantage of. They especially don't
want to talk about their shortcomings or weaknesses.

— They are great manipulators when it comes to controlling
their partner. They do not want to admit that they are
seeking proof of their partner's love. They will stop at nothing to manipulate the other person: sulking, blackmailing,
lying, seducing, crying with rage, yelling, threatening and
complaining. They can even resort to violence.

— They understand and act quickly, but most of the time, they
do so, having jumped to conclusions too quickly.

— They are convinced they are right, attempt to impose their
views on others and like to have the last word.

— They are spiteful. They can break off a relationship abruptly
without notice and refuse all contact for a long period.

— They are intolerant and impatient with people they consider too slow. They make no secret of their anger.

— They project themselves as being very independent so as not to trigger their fear of separation or abandonment. They criticize dependent people.

— They often use the following expressions: I am able, you can count on me, I don't trust him, I knew it, I was right, did you understand, listen to me; and the following words: associated, disassociated, separated, left, it's true, well, really!, etc.

Description of the physical body:

— The man shows strength and power in the upper body, and his shoulders are therefore wider than his hips.

— The woman's hips and/or upper thighs are wider and stronger than her shoulders. That part of the body radiates strength.

— Dominant muscles in several parts of the body.

— Strong voice.

— The man has a large and strong chest.

— Looks strong but not fat, if overweight.

— Inclined to have a bigger belly with age.

— Large eyes with an intense, seductive look.

— Likes flamboyant clothing.

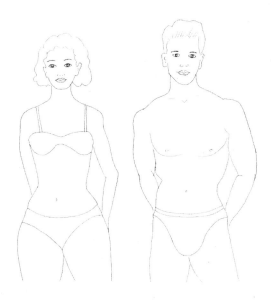

Body of a person suffering
from the wound of BETRAYAL
(Controler mask)

Wound of injustice

Awakening of the wound: between the ages of four and six with the parent of the same sex.

This is a child who had a chilly relationship with the parent of the same sex. They were unable to express and be themselves with this parent. They reacted by cutting themselves off from their sensitivity, made it a point to perform and to be perfect. They prevented the expression of their individuality.

Mask: Rigidity

Greatest fear: Coldness

Attitudes and behaviours of the wound when the mask is activated:

— *Rigid* people strive to appear lively and dynamic, even if they are tired.

— They rarely admit they are having problems or that something is bothering them. If they admit to a problem, they are quick to add it is not serious or that they are or were able to get through it alone.

— They are highly optimistic and always want to show they are positive.

— They control themselves to be perfect and to match the ideal they have set for themselves or which they believe people expect of them.

— They go to great lengths to control their anger – that which they are aware of – as they are fearful of losing control.

— They may seem controlling with others when their own perfection is questioned and when they are defending themselves.

— Although they want everything to be perfect and fair, they are often the first ones to exaggerate a fact or an accusation. They are unaware just how unfair they can be to others and to themselves.

— *Rigid* people do not want to feel. They have trouble showing their feelings, because they do not know how to manage their great sensitivity. They fear losing control and not being perfect in the eyes of others.

- They come across as cold and insensitive, because they have convinced both themselves and others that nothing affects them. As a result, they are unable to establish a satisfying intimate relationship.

- They are very hard on their body and rarely admit they are sick. They do not feel cold or pain very much. They take great pride in not needing medication or having to visit a doctor.

- They feel appreciated especially by what they do and how they look. They do not stop until everything has been done and is perfect. Before indulging in pleasure, they must deserve it by having worked hard.

- They demand much of themselves, want to perform and reach beyond their boundaries. They have disdain for lazy people.

- They are good at engaging in self-sabotage when things start going too well, in their estimation.

- Everything must be fair, justified and justifiable. When someone finds fault with them, justification is immediately forthcoming. They can lie to justify themselves, and if they fear getting caught at lying, they prepare their justification in advance.

- They cannot prevent themselves from interrupting someone who has said something wrong, thinking that they are being of help. They readily criticize everyone who does not act in a way they believe to be perfect and fair, and they are just as critical of themselves.

- They believe that knowledge is more important than feelings. They are immensely proud of their knowledge and their memory.

— When they have reached their limit, they can be biting, sarcastic, hard-headed and unyielding.

— They often use the following words: no problem, exactly, surely, always, never, correct, supposed, it must, I should, extraordinary, fantastic, along with all of the superlatives such as: just great, very special, really nice, etc.

Description of the physical body:

— Well proportioned body, as perfect as possible.

— Very straight posture.

— Square shoulders.

— Parts of the body that are rigid, stiff. (e.g., legs, neck, back, etc.)

— Abrupt movements.

— Cared-for and seductive appearance.

— Small waist tightened with clothing or a belt.

— Clenched jaw.

— Flat chest they try to pull in.

— Round, bulging buttocks.

— Clear, radiant complexion.

— Bright, lively and direct look.

— Curt and fast voice.

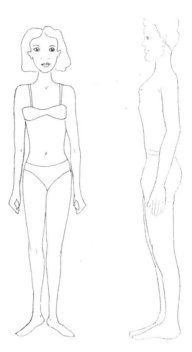

*Body of a person suffering
from the wound of INJUSTICE
(Mask of Rigidity)*

Activating the wounds

The attitudes and behaviours cited in the description of each mask manifest themselves when the wound is activated and we decide to wear the mask associated with the particular wound. We wear a mask because our ego believes that by resorting to these various behaviours, we will not feel the hurt caused by the activated wound. We also believe that the others will not see our wound.

This can also be compared with covering up a physical wound with a bandage or swallowing a pill in order to avoid exposing ourselves to pain. By doing so, we are pretending there is no pain. Physical pain is the reflection of psychological pain and attracts our attention to the real cause of the harm.

This book provides you with the ways and means to eradicate the harm yourself. Do note, however, that you must do more than just read about it. You will have to learn to put into practice the various tools you will come across, and in so doing, you will gradually lessen the pain yourself, with no need for outside help.

Healing a wound of the soul can be compared to healing a physical injury. For example, someone who can easily find a message relating to a physical malaise has gone through various learning phases. At the beginning, they are unaware and totally dependent on outside help (medication or a therapist). They then clue into the fact there is a message that extends beyond the physical harm, and while taking medication or receiving assistance to obtain relief, they attempt to decode the message. With time, they discover the message more quickly and end up not needing outside help.

A wound is activated or affected in one of three ways, as was mentioned earlier in the triangle of life. They are as follows:

1. You are affected by the attitude or behaviour that someone has directed toward you.

2. You are feeling guilty towards someone because of what you say or do or what you plan to say or do, being afraid of wounding them and activating one of their wounds.

3. You suffer because of what you are doing to yourself or how you are toward yourself.

Every day, we move from one wound to another, depending on the circumstances and the persons we associate with. Generally speaking, I have noted that, in the workplace, we suffer from rejection and injustice more often, whereas in our personal lives, abandonment and betrayal are encountered more frequently. Humiliation is always experienced with oneself. We do not accuse people of humiliating us. This will be explained further in the chapter on humiliation.

Now that I have read this chapter, this is what I have decided to apply to my life:

_____

_____

_____

_____

_____

_____

_____

_____

_____

_____

_____

_____

_____

_____

Chapter Two

Common questions

This chapter deals with the questions that are regularly asked about the 5 wounds in the workshops and conferences of the *Listen to Your Body* School.

Are adopted children to conclude that it was their biological parents rather than their adoptive parents who were the first ones to activate their wounds?

Our wounds are initially activated from conception to the age of seven. Some movements in psychology maintain that we have already developed all of our beliefs during the first seven years of our lives. It is certain that most of our beliefs, fears, feelings and decisions are experienced unconsciously.

When it comes to activating our wounds, biological parents or adoptive parents can be the trigger. In addition, everyone who has played the role of a parent during the first seven years of life has activated the wounds that already existed before we were born. These people could be a grandparent, a babysitter, a teacher or any important person.

I have encountered numerous instances of adopted persons who, as adults, managed to locate their biological parents. After meeting with them and spending time with them to know them better, they were quite surprised to discover how similar their wounds were – and the same holds for their emotions, fears and beliefs.

An adopted child, even one who has never met their biological parents, will always share a very profound link to them for having chosen them for incarnation. Their genetic link is as important as the link between their souls.

If you were adopted, do not forget that experiencing rejection and abandonment from birth is part of your life plan to help you accept these wounds in this life. You will have great difficulty healing them until such time as you take responsibility for this choice.

Right from birth, people looking after a child will act and react to them, based on what they have to learn together. Absolutely nothing is left to chance. Life is imbued with such intelligence that accepting this fact is imperative. How many times have I heard a mom tell me with emotion in her voice, *"I don't know why I flip out so easily with my second daughter. She has a knack of getting me going, and I forget all of my good intentions to be tolerant of her. I don't get it, as I never experienced that with her elder sister who is only three years older than her."*

In this example, the wounds are activated in both the child and the mother. The mother loses control, because she feels rejected by her daughter. She then accuses herself of being a bad mother (wounds of rejection and injustice) and she angrily lashes out. This type of reaction can be triggered even when the daughter doesn't say a word: all it takes is a look or a certain movement. This clearly shows that suffering comes from our interpretation of a situation. A wound activated in one person indicates that the same wound was activated in the other, at the same time and to the same degree. That applies equally to an adopted child.

I wish to point out here that there is no need to know when and by whom our wounds were activated during our childhood. The important thing is to acknowledge their existence. As we become more aware and are able to accept ourselves more, some events in the distant past become easier to recall.

If the father or mother were not around when we were kids, does that mean some wounds were not activated?

No, unfortunately, it does not. I know some would like to enjoy such fortune, but such is not the case.

For example, a mother who was alone to take care of her daughter, with no one else around to play the father role, had a child who was affected by wounds of abandonment and betrayal.

The injuries can be activated in various ways:

— By what the mother had to day about the absent father.

— By what the daughter observed in other fathers and their children.

— By an older brother or any other man in the family.

— By the image of a father she created in her mind.

— By any man who could represent a father in her eyes, such as a teacher or a family friend.

The same applies to those who had only one parent during their childhood and adolescence.

> *My mother died when I was three,*
> *and my father remarried when I was*
> *six. Of the two moms I had, which one*
> *activated my wounds the most?*

In a blended family, everyone who plays the role of a parent has an influence on you. In general, the biological parent activates more profound wounds, but the new parent very often continues activating them.

Remember that we always attract to ourselves the persons we need at each important moment of our life.

Must homosexuals invert the role of parents?

No. It doesn't matter if it is woman or a man. It has nothing to do with wounds. Sexual preference is something that is very personal and solely physical, even though their choice was made in reaction to one of their parents.

It bears repeating—the important thing is not finding out who was the first person to activate certain wounds; it is recognizing that these wounds are ours and that our parents were chosen based on their life plan which is linked to ours. They always participate in our spiritual development.

The reaction to someone's choice of homosexuality has a direct link with what they have to learn. In general, if the parents readily accept it, this reflects their own acceptance and the wounds are not activated in this area of their life. If, however, one or both parents are not accepting, this triggers one or several wounds. They can be determined by looking at the description of each one.

As far as the partners are concerned, it is true that this can cause confusion at times. For example, when two women are living together, one can play the woman's role more, and the other person the male role. If that is your particular case and you are considered the woman in the couple, your partner can revive suffering you experienced with your father and with your mother. I suggest that you do not look too hard to find out. All you have to do is manage each wound as it is triggered, which will set you on the path to a better relationship. If you are comfortable with choosing to live as a homosexual, you will certainly be confronted by less confusion and be better able to manage the emotions you experience.

I also often hear that heterosexual couples encounter confusion as well. A woman can say that her husband is exactly like her mother and wonders how to interpret the wounds. She need only focus on the behaviour influenced byte mask at play, and the wound relating to it. Then when she decides to go deeper and ask herself what she judges her spouse of BEING, she will end up discovering that she accused her father of BEING the same thing. The confusion often stems from the fact that the behaviour is different, even though the accusation is the same. I will delve into this later in the book.

> ***There is increasing talk of transsexuals, transgenders, intersexuals and so on. Who must they consider to activate their wounds?***

The answer is always the same. Our parents - or those who played the role of a parent - will always activate our wounds without realizing it so that we become aware of what we have to learn. The same can be said for our parents who need us for their soul to evolve.

When someone chooses a life that doesn't fit the mould, they are more inclined to experience rejection from others and from themselves. However, millions of people come into this world sporting a major wound of rejection, even though they appear to be living on the straight and narrow. It is preferable that all of us not get too bogged down with differences and focus instead on appeasing our suffering. No one else can do it for us.

> ### *What happens when we turn to a surrogate mother? Who is the child affected by in terms of their wounds?*

During the nine months of gestation, the link is very strong, because the baby is totally dependent on the surrogate mother. They are therefore influenced by what they live and feel. Since there is no coincidence involved, the woman who is available to bear this baby will influence the latter, depending on what the baby's soul needs to feel and learn from that woman. Since the child will then lose all contact with her, they will quickly forget their start to life and live the experiences they will need with the mother who will be present.

This kind of experience can be handled in very different ways. Some babies can feel rejected, others abandoned, and some others feeling a sense of injustice, and so on. Some can even consider that this method of fertilization is proof that their birth was much desired.

> **Today, you can conceive children by in vitro fertilization. How does that affect the wounds?**

Once again, it is important to bear in mind that there is no such thing as luck or coincidence and that everything is programmed before we are born according to our life plan. It is sure that if the father's sperm fertilizes the mother's egg, one can conclude that everything is occurring like any normal pregnancy, except for the major efforts that have been made. The parents, in particular, can wonder what this experience has to teach them. The child, meanwhile, will know they are very much desired, which cannot be said for everyone.

In vitro fertilization can also be achieved using the sperm of an unknown donor. In this case, the child will come away feeling the same as if they had a father who was absent or who had disappeared.

In cases where the father's sperm is used to impregnate a surrogate mother, refer to the question dealing with the surrogate mother.

The most important thing to bear in mind is that, regardless of the circumstances, the child's soul and the parents' souls needed this experience to evolve based on their life plan.

Only the ego believes that our suffering is caused by others. As long as we hold onto the belief that we are the victims, no spiritual journey is possible.

> ## *You say that each of us has the four wounds, except the wound of humiliation. Why is it that I am the only one in my family to have it?*

When I say all of us have four out of five, that does not mean the soul does not have to accept the wound of humiliation. We all have a genetic memory inherited from our family and a cellular memory accumulated during the numerous lives our soul has lived. All of these lives are useful in learning to accept everything that can be experienced on this great Planet Earth. During some lives, we also experience the wound of humiliation to verify the extent of our acceptance.

The person who asked this question believed they were the only one in their family to suffer from it. If they took the time to go through their genealogical history, they would possibly find someone who greatly resembles them and who was also affected.

My intuition tells me that when someone closely resembles their great-grandfather, for example, it is the same soul that reincarnated in order to complete the acceptance that was not achieved previously.

I frequently see people who cannot accept the wound of humiliation inflicted by one of their family members, who say things like, *Why do you let people take advantage of you like that? You're too good-natured!"* or *"Why do you allow yourself to get that big? You should go on a diet!*

If you see yourself criticizing – either verbally or in thought – people who have a weight problem who have several characteristics of the masochist mask, you know right then you have not yet accepted the behaviours and physical appearance of the wound of humiliation. This may begin to manifest itself later in your life, or it could be deferred to a future life.

The same applies to people who have only one part of the body that is round, for example the face or the legs, but no other visible sign of that wound. If they control themselves to avoid putting on weight by using their rigidity mask, they have not yet reached the acceptance process.

It is so much wiser to directly confront the lessons we have to learn. Not only do we thus avoid living the same thing over and over in future lives, but the greatest benefit of accepting oneself and others is the happiness we feel.

Do twins necessarily have the same wounds?

Until only recently, it was believed that fraternal twins were two separate beings each with their own personalities and that identical twins were identical in every respect, from their appearance to their nature. Some scientists are now saying that identical twins are not 100% identical, especially in terms of the lifestyle adopted and the illnesses they get. For example, researchers fail to understand why one twin gets cancer at a very young age and the other twin only at age 70.

A great deal of research has been done on twins, and I suggest that you refer to the information on the Internet to find out more.

Given the law of cause and effect that states we shape our lives by our decisions and actions, it is easy to understand why twins live different experiences, even though their bodies seem to be identical.

The choices they make all their lives are what make the difference. If one decides to become more aware to appease their suffering, in other words, if they prefer love to fear, acceptance to resistance, thereby allowing their heart to guide their life instead of their ego, it is certain they will have fewer illnesses than the twin who chooses to listen to their ego.

I have observed that if one identical twin adopts a new behaviour, it is highly likely the other twin will follow suit. They are so intermingled that they feel each other easily, even if they are some distance apart. It would seem that the one born first has more influence on the other, but since all of us have freedom of choice, it is impossible to predict with certainty how identical twins will conduct themselves.

Now that I have read this chapter, this is what I have decided to apply to my life:

_____

_____

_____

_____

_____

_____

_____

_____

_____

_____

_____

_____

_____

_____

_____

_____

Chapter Three

Ego – the greatest obstacle to healing

When writing the title of this chapter, I wondered why ego is gaining increasing recognition, given that many authors have already written extensively about it. The answer that came to mind was that this very awakening of collective awareness is the reason why the ego is still very much alive – it's doing all that it can to stay alive and strong.

I continue to talk about it, as I do in every one of my books and in each one of the *Listen to Your Body* workshops and conferences. For those who have read several of my books or attended workshops, I thought I would add many examples to this chapter and throughout the book. I want to help you even more to realize exactly when you are managing your own life and at what point you allow your ego to take control.

In the past 45 years, I have read thousands of books and taken part in numerous training sessions to develop my personal awareness. Moreover, I have been teaching for more than 30 years. Even with all of this experience, I am still discovering things I was previously unaware of, and each discovery leaves me agape. Every time, I am surprised that whatever I have just learned never dawned on me beforehand.

That is why I really want to help you discover, through this book, the tremendous influence, grasp and power that your ego can have on you. I am sure I am not the only one who has become gradually more aware each passing day, week and year.

EGO – The greatest obstacle to healing the 5 wounds

After wondering quite often whether it is possible that I will no longer be influenced by my ego one day, I decided to let go and just bask in the joy that washes over me when I realize all the ways it tricks me and guides me. That's the only way I will manage to get better control over my life.

Creating ego

I am often asked: *Where does ego come from? Why is it so important to all of our lives?* Ego began to manifest itself when humans developed their mental energy several million years ago. Remember the story of *Adam and Eve?* They lived in paradise on Earth. When Eve ate the apple from the tree of knowledge (mental dimension), they became imperfect, and problems began to emerge.

This symbolism tells us that, with the mental energy humans have developed, we have inherited the power of choice. We are the only creatures on Earth who enjoy free will. Over time, we have chosen to give a lot of space to our mental dimension and used its energy to create our ego, believing that it would be useful to us; however, we have allowed it to usurp our power. Unfortunately, we ended up forgetting that the only real power we have is the divine being in each one of us – our light, our great wisdom.

Ego can be compared to a neighbour whom we have given leeway to come over to our home to tell us how to live our lives. In this scenario, the neighbour would feel extremely important and indispensable. He would be convinced we could not live without him, and that if left to our own devices, we would be unable to make any decisions in our lives. Could we really blame the neighbour? The answer is no, because he thinks he is doing us a favour.

The same goes for our ego. It cannot see itself or realize what is really happening. That is why we must learn to observe ourselves to become aware of its presence. It is similar to a stain on a canvas that doesn't know it is a stain. We have to take a step back and look at the canvas to see the stain.

It is very important to bear in mind that ego consists of mental energy. Our mental dimension is crucial to our ability to think, reason, plan, organize, memorize, and so on. It is subtle matter that we can neither see, nor touch – the antithesis of our physical dimension – but is nonetheless omnipresent and important. In order to be able to think and organize, our mental dimension must always rely on its memory, on everything it learned in the past. Our mental dimension is content and balanced when it is using everything it learned to help us respond to the needs of our being.

So why do I want to talk so much about ego in this book? It is of utmost importance, because it will help you become more aware of all the times when one of your wounds is provoked and you react. Every reaction is brought on by a provoked wound, and this always reflects the grasp ego has on us.

> **When you realize that your ego has taken over, you know right away that you are wearing a mask associated with one of your wounds.**

What is the ego?

Ego is entirely a human creation and feeds off our mental energy to survive. It relies solely on everything that has been learned in the past. For example, any situation it believes to be a hazard when it was experienced in the past will continue to be considered a hazard for evermore, as long as we allow it to.

It constantly seeks to stop things in their tracks, while denying change in every possible way. Suffering is one of its specialties.

> **The ego suffers due to unfulfilled desires and also out of fear of suffering if its desires materialize.**

It cannot live in reality, because it compares everything to the world it created. It is convinced its own world is the real world. How many times have I heard adults tell me about hard times they experienced in childhood, all the while convinced they were real. After checking with their family, they realized their perception was false, that no one else had lived and perceived the situation the same way. The suffering these events created stayed with them for many years, because their ego influenced them to perceive things its way rather than see reality.

I come from a family of 11, and I'm sure that if you asked each one of us one after the other to describe our parents, we would each have a different version. When I was young, a fire broke out at our house, and several years later, this came up during a conversation between my sisters and me. We talked about the fire, and none of us had the same version of events. All of us experienced a different fire. That is the kind of influence our beliefs, our fears and our ego can have on us.

Since the ego is created with mental matter, it can be considered a mental outgrowth. You are certainly familiar with the physical outgrowth of the body such as warts, cysts, tumors, etc. They are made of physical matter but are not natural. They parasitize the body and milk it for energy to create themselves and continue to exist. Their structure has always fascinated me. They even manage to develop small blood vessels to survive longer.

The ego, which is similar, causes much more damage, because it has its own will to live and survive. It lives in constant fear of dying, disappearing, as if it knew that, in fact, it is short-lived and not real, just as we ourselves are. At the same time, it is unaware of this, and that it is why it strives to convince itself of its existence.

Its ignorance is similar to that of someone who does not admit they are afraid of running out of money. They convince themselves by spending a lot and telling anyone within earshot they really feel sure about themselves, that they are not afraid of running short and that they'll always have money to pay off their debts. They'll even go so far as to criticize or attempt to change people that appear to be financially insecure. We all know that if they weren't afraid, they would not have to convince others or even themselves. The same goes for the ego that always attempts to convince itself it exists, though, in actual fact, it is but an illusion.

The ego weakens you, because it saps your mental energy. Every time you allow it to control you, your energy wanes. I am sure you've noticed this many times. When you experience fears and emotions–which are manifestations of the ego—you've certainly realized you're tired at the end of the day. Only you can decide whether or not you are going to go on feeding your ego. Sadly, it's not that easy, because we've given it a great deal of power throughout numerous lifetimes. It has found subtle ways of tricking us and making us believe we make the decisions in our lives, when in fact we let our ego take over.

The ego : the sum total of your beliefs

You've certainly noted hundreds of these little voices talking incessantly to you, scaring you, causing you to doubt yourself or others, making you feel guilty, preventing you from taking action, making you distort reality, etc. Every little voice is linked to one of your beliefs. The more you keep them going by caving into them, the more importance they gain. In short, the ego is the sum total of these beliefs that prevent you from being yourself. When I make reference to a part of the ego, I am referring to one of the beliefs that make up your ego.

The difficulty of regaining control

Why is it so difficult to regain control of our lives and not allow the ego to control us? The main reason is the lack of awareness that each of us has. We are aware of only between 5% and 10% of what is going on inside of us. That means we are barely conscious of the many times when the hundreds of beliefs we possess manage our lives.

I do hope that after reading this book, you will have an eas-ier time realizing this quickly. To do so, it is imperative you bear in mind that the ego, the little me, only thinks of itself and that it will continue to exist throughout its continual thoughts of ME, MYSELF AND I. That is its way of proving it exists. It seems to believe it is alone in its battle with the entire world.

> **The ego has an incessant need to convince itself that it exists and that it is so important that it can continue to exist eternally, just like humans.**

Let us take a look together at a typical day in the life of a married woman with two adolescents, who holds down a job. Most of the following examples can apply just as easily to a man.

Everything in italics below represents the thoughts of her little me (ego) that is afraid for her image, afraid of not being loved, not being recognized, making a mistake, etc. It's that ego again that keeps driving home that ME... I ....

She oversleeps. *Damned alarm clock! How come it didn't go off? I'M gonna be late. The boss is going to give ME a nasty look again.*

She joins her husband and two children into the kitchen. *How come you didn't wake ME up? Seems to ME I told you yesterday that I had to leave earlier this morning.*

She hurries to get ready, but can't find the outfit she wants to wear. *Dammit, it's still at the cleaners! If I didn't have to do so much in the house, I'd have had time to pick it up yesterday.*

She looks at herself in the mirror. *Another wrinkle! Boy is family life making ME age fast. I'd need to take a vacation more often. I'm getting more unsightly by the day, and I look older than my elder sister.*

She ducks into the washroom before heading out. *Here we go again. Someone left the toilet seat up. I'm sure my husband* did. Men don't think about WE women. When will they under-stand it's impolite?

While driving into work: *Look at that bloody slowpoke hold-ing up traffic and delaying ME. What's he doing on the road at this hour?*

She arrives late for work: *Sorry for being late. Everything was against ME this morning. To start with, MY husband...* And she goes on to explain everything to justify herself.

At a meeting: *Why do I have to waste MY time listening to the same old thing over and over? I thought it was an import-ant meeting. Why is she always the one doing the talking? Why am I not asked for MY opinion? They mustn't respect me.*

She goes to a restaurant for lunch: *Fries again. I promised MYSELF that I'd stop eating them. I'm gonna get even fatter. I've got no willpower!*

She goes and gets her fourth coffee of the day. *That'll be MY last one for the day. I know it's too much, but everyone is getting on MY nerves today, and I need even more.*

Her boss brings her some work she was not expecting to get. *How come I'm the one that ends up with the extra work? At least if she said a little thanks to ME once in a while, it'd be encouraging. What in God's name did I ever do to be swamped like this here and at home? Everybody is taking advantage of ME.*

She arrives late to drive her son to his football practice. *Don't look at ME that way, and don't say anything. I am doing MY best. You don't know what it's like having to do everything at home and work outside as well.*

She gets home. Her husband arrived earlier than usual. *There he is parked in front of the TV. Couldn't he have thought of preparing ME a nice surprise and fixing dinner tonight instead of ME?*

Her son arrives late from his football practice. She gets upset that she has to prepare him something to eat. *Couldn't you have told ME that you'd be late for dinner? I thought you were at your friend's house. I get the impression everybody thinks I'm a servant around here.*

She finally plunks herself down in front of the TV at 9 pm to watch a series on the story of four different women at home. *Gee I'd like to live in a beautiful house like that and have a maid do everything in the house for ME! Did you see the other one and the nice clothes she was wearing? Not only that, she doesn't even have to work to afford it all. What's the use of dreaming? I'd never be lucky enough to have a lifestyle like that one day.*

Her son and daughter get into an argument, and the tone becomes increasingly heated. *I can't stand listening to you two any longer. I'm tired, I've had a hard day. Couldn't you not think of others once in a while? I need to relax. I've just sat down, and I've been grinding all day.*

Her husband wants to make love. *How come he can't get it through his head that with everything I've got to do, I don't have any energy left to make love? Men are all the same. That's all they think of, and they ignore our needs. So I'll give in, end of story. I'll have a few days' peace and he'll be nicer with me tomorrow.*

ATTENTION: I'm not telling you to stop using the words *I* or *me*. For example, if you are telling someone about an incident, you'll probably use those words quite often. We know the ego took over when we can hear hidden criticism in the sentence, a feeling of superiority or search for attention or compliments.

The ego uses criticism

The ego uses a very subtle ruse to control us and give us importance by often directing criticism to others and passing it off as observations. You read a few examples in the last few pages. The ego likes to find fault with others to convince itself that it is better and more important than others. When we are aware of criticizing, we think the person deserves it, because, in our estimation they are really the ones who are wrong.

I must admit that having discovered and continuing to see aspects of my ego every day is one of the great revelations of my life. The more aware I become, the more I discover just how all-encompassing it is. The big advantage of making this discovery is that the very instant I become aware I'm not the one managing my life, I am able to put an immediate end to my ego's influence.

> **If you really want to lessen and gradually heal your wounds, it is imperative that you become aware of the tremendous power and influence your ego has in your life.**

When you accept the fact that any manifestation of the ego shows us that one of our wounds has been activated, it then becomes imperative that you be aware of its presence. Here is one way that can help you develop this awareness. For every example of criticism, whether verbalized or in thought, I have added some egotistical thoughts.

— *Did you see how fat she has gotten? Does she not have a mirror at home? (I would never let MYSELF get that way. I have more willpower than she does).*

— *He never stops talking. He just takes over the floor. Doesn't he realize that the others would also like to talk? (I am more discreet and attentive to other people's needs).*

— *What's that fool doing on the road? He cut ME off and almost plowed into ME. How come he has a driver's licence? (I drive a lot better than that – I'd never do that).*

— *Poor thing, it's one problem after another, and she is becoming more and more of a victim. (I take charge of MY life, I don't seek attention through MY problems. I don't take advantage of other people like she does).*

— *I'm fed up always having to repeat things. Seems to ME what I'm saying is clear! (I listen better, I'm more attentive and quick to catch on to everything).*

— *I just don't get why she keeps acting this way, even though she knows I don't like it. (I take into consideration what she likes – it's the least I can do to show MY love for her).*

— *I hate calling an administrative office. First of all, we have to spend several minutes talking to a machine, and when we finally get through to a person, they ask us all the same questions. It's just so time-consuming. (If I were the one in charge, I'd think about the customers and I'd change the entire system. I'm sure I'd find one that would be better).*

— *Why do you ask me for my opinion when you never like any of MY answers and you just go on doing what you want to* do anyway? (*I'm not egotistical like that. I'm more flexible and I don't waste other people's time*).

— How can a man put up with doing such a dirty job? (*I think too much of myself to allow MYSELF to do something like that. I'm worthy of a more honourable trade*).

— How come it is taking so long for ME to be served? There aren't many people in the restaurant. Are the servers on strike? (*If I were the owner, you could bet that service would become a priority.*)

— I can't figure out why restaurants are serving us food in plastic containers. Talk about pollution! The poor planet is awash in garbage! (*I've evolved more – I know the consequences of such pollution.*)

— No wonder he has health problems. He hardly drinks any water which is the body's second greatest need. (*I'm smarter, and I drink a lot of water, as I'm supposed to.*)

— He's been living with the same problems for years, and several of us have suggested solutions to him. When will he consider them? I don't feel like helping him anymore. (*I'd be so grateful to have people like ME and want to help ME that I'd do something to change.*

— I really think it's too bad that MY sister seems to prefer her son to her daughter. She's really unfair (*I'd never act that way with my children. I love them too much to do something like that.*)

— I don't understand why MY parents continue living together. They're always arguing, and MY father always has to cave in to MY mother (*If I were like my mother and never happy with what my spouse does for me, I'd leave him or if I were my father, I'd be stronger than him and never allow MYSELF to be controlled like that by MY wife.)*

— *Every time I see my mother, she tells me all about my sister's accomplishments. Why can't she compliment ME instead? (I am not unfair like she is.)*

The ego uses superlatives

Every time we exaggerate, the ME, MYSELF and I is seeking even greater recognition. It uses superlatives such as *always, never* or any other form of exaggeration.

— *You are ALWAYS busy at work, even at the house, and you're NEVER there when I need you.*

— *I NEVER eat dessert.*

— *You're ALWAYS late.*

— *I no longer have any fears.*

— *You NEVER understand anything. I ALWAYS have to repeat myself.*

— *MY son ALWAYS lies to me.*

— *I'M ALWAYS the one who has to work overtime.*

— *You NEVER talk to me. When you come home from work, you ALWAYS plunk yourself down in front of the TV before and after dinner.*

The ego uses "I have to" or the conditional tense

Whether in thought or words, the ego uses expressions such as I HAVE TO or verbs in the conditional tense such as *I should* or *I would like to, it would be nice, etc.*

The ego does this because these formulations are expressions of fear, even though it is hidden. By limiting us in this way, the ego is convincing us once again to listen to its fears.

Let's look at a few examples: *I HAVE TO stop eating so much* or *I HAVE TO stop smoking.* The ego wants to instill fear and control, once again, to feel it exists and that it is powerful. It does not know that we always have a choice in life. It especially doesn't know that when we make a decision based on fear, we are feeding into that fear, and it ends up manifesting itself more and more. It does not realize it is asking us to control ourselves to avoid something. However, the control is the best way for this something to manifest itself rather than disappear.

All of these expressions in the conditional tense conceal an unconscious fear. *I SHOULD tell my colleague at work that I am fed up with his disparaging remarks about me. Would I ever LIKE TO be able to answer him in the same tone of voice.* Several fears can be hiding behind that desire phrased in the conditional tense. If the person weren't afraid, they'd say instead, *That's it. I've decided that I'll be talking to my colleague tomorrow. I need to straighten things out with him to have a better working relationship.*

The ego identifies with "having" and "doing."

Because the ego identifies with what it has and does, it wants to own everything that feeds it and makes it feel secure, such as things and people. It does not want to lose anything, because it would believe it is losing a part of itself. Another instance is when someone makes every attempt to squeeze into a conversation what they own or by showing it off in every way imaginable.

> **You are not what you own (things, money, talent, titles) and you're not what you do (job, parent, etc.)**

Several years ago, I met someone who always bought very luxurious cars. When we'd go out to a restaurant, he'd give the doorman a hefty tip to park his car right beside the restaurant! On the other hand, he could go several kilometers out of his way to buy dog food or toilet paper on discount. He'd go to these lengths to pinch pennies, and yet he'd spend outrageously on something else. I realized one day that he identified himself with his cars. *If I have a nice car and I give people the impression I'm wealthy, I AM somebody.* This particular fellow was wealthy for several years but lived out the last years of his life penniless and heavily in debt.

An attitude like this tricks the ego into believing it is important and that it really does exist. Bear in mind, though, that down deep, the ego knows it's short-lived and that it must always find ways to convince itself it exists and especially that it will continue to exist.

When someone loses their fortune and their company goes bankrupt, prompting them to think suicide is the solution, it means that they identified with "having" and "doing."

It is easy to spot someone who identifies with their trade. They jump right away into talking about what they do for a living as soon as they meet somebody, without even being asked the question. *I'm a doctor, engineer, author or the director of a large company.* People like this bask in the admiration or recognition they receive from others. If they receive special privileges because of their title or their trade, they swell with happiness. Their ego rises at the same rate as they feed it.

Many women even identify with what their spouse does for a living. *I'm Mrs. So-and-so, Dr. Grenier's wife. Or I'm the sister of x, you know the guy who won the silver medal at the Olympics?*

Have you noticed how often you or people in your surroundings use possessive terms when talking about your things, the people close to you or yourselves? Here are a few examples.

— *Hi Lise, I'd like to introduce you to MY husband. When I hear this, I feel like responding in jest, "Hi, MY HUSBAND," because she never told me his first name!*

— *MY child, MY mother, MY father, MY sister, instead of the person's first name, or MY dad, MY mom.*

— *I ask about the health of a friend I haven't seen in several months, and she answers: MY backache is getting worse, and so are MY migraines. And I have just learned I'm in the early stages of diabetes. What did I do to God to bring so many problems onto myself? And when will He leave me be?*

— *MY money, MY jewelry, MY bank account...*

— *Who put this big scratch on MY nice new car?* No need to add MY car. *Who put this big scratch* would have been enough.

- You are waiting in line to take the bus, and someone tries to sneak in ahead of you. You angrily shove the person, *That's MY spot. No way are you butting in ahead of ME!*

- While out for a walk with her husband, a woman snuggles up to him, with a look on her face that says to any women nearby, *See how important I am. I'm lucky enough to have a man like him who loves ME! He's all MINE, just so you know! (Men do the same thing).*

This can even become jealousy which is a major manifestation of ego. A jealous person cannot imagine someone else taking THEIR possession away. And what about you? What are you afraid of losing? Your reply indicates you believe you are what you own. Remember, though, that you are allowing yourself to be influenced by your ego.

Someone who identifies with what they do has a lot of difficulty accepting criticism. They quickly conclude that the criticism is directed at who they ARE and do not even realize that it is aimed instead at what they are DOING. Here are some examples of criticisms with the interpretation by the ego of the person for whom the criticism was intended.

- *That new dish is rather tasteless. (It figures. I'M a lousy cook.)*

- *My friend's mom is not always criticizing him. (I'M a bad mother). My friend's dad takes time out to play with him. (I'M a bad father).*

- *You've been making the same mistake for three years now. How long will it take for you to get it through your head? (I'M a dummy, not worth a damn).*

Here are some of the comments that my teachers and I hear sometimes after conferences and workshops. *Your conference was too long. The solutions didn't have enough detail. We didn't have enough time for some exercises. You finished too late. You didn't answer the questions from everyone who raised their hand, and so on.*

If we overlooked the fact these people were only referring to some details regarding how we teach, our ego would take over, and the attendant thoughts would take over such as: *Well, that says it all. I'm a lousy teacher. People don't like me. Perhaps I'm gonna lose my job.* Besides, that is why we ask participants to be kind enough to give us their comments on what should be kept and/or changed for each workshop. That helps us accept the fact that meeting everyone's expectations is impossible. This applies to all areas of life. When criticism is levelled at us, our ego causes us to forget what we did well and to disregard all of the compliments paid to us by others.

Do you know a child who has never compared his parents to other parents or to a teacher? Even if they like the behaviour of their friend's parent more, that does not mean the child doesn't love their mother or father. They are only referring to a behaviour and not to what his parents ARE.

The ego seeks out compliments

Do you know how your ego goes about getting compliments?

> **The ego loves compliments and recognition and stops at nothing to get them. It does this to reinforce the feeling it exists and that it is important. The ego believes it is invincible.**

Here are several examples:

— Telling the people close to you what you did during the day without them asking you.

— Spending a lot of time choosing clothing and fussing over your physical appearance in the hope of being noticed.

— Loading up on knowledge to get the last word in, convinced that you know more than other people do.

— Running on about your past exploits.

— Complaining about your weaknesses or putting yourself down, hoping to hear others respond that you are or are doing a lot better than you think.

— Revealing the price of something expensive you bought (without the other person asking you what you paid).

— Wanting your children or your grandchildren to visit you more often in recognition of everything you have done for them.

— Offering to pick up the tab for everyone at the restaurant, when you know you can't afford to.

— Going regularly to the same restaurant or to the same vacation spot to be recognized by the employees. Being flattered when they remember your first name and your preferences.

You may even say you never fish for compliments which you claim make you feel uncomfortable. It is highly likely that when someone actually does, you answer right away that you're not that way. For example, *"I think you're really well*

organized to have managed to submit this project on time."
Your answer: "No, I didn't do it all by myself. I got help, and I'm
not as well organized as you may think." An answer like that
indicates that you may even be fishing for more compliments,
because you believe you must be exceptional to be entitled
to compliments from other people. You would like the other
person to insist on this quality, which would satisfy your ego. If
not, you would have simply said, "Thank you very much. That's
very nice of you."

The ego doesn't listen

The following is a list of examples, showing another very
common characteristic of the ego – the inability to listen. It
jumps to conclusions. It takes over the conversation when we
are talking to someone or it interrupts to take over the floor.

— Someone asks your sister how many hours she sleeps at
   night. She answers, and you hasten to add, "ME, I sleep
   about seven hours a night."

— A friend simply speaks to you about a problem they are
   having, and you immediately conclude they have asked
   you for help: I've got the solution for you. You should do
   this or that. I suggest that you follow MY advice. I'm sure
   that'll work.

— Or you could interrupt the friend and say, The same thing
   happened to ME last year. I did such-and-such, and I know
   you could do the same thing I did and probably end up with
   the same results.

— During one of our teacher meetings, one of them raised
   her hand to share a good idea that came to mind during
   a workshop. No sooner had she stopped talking when

another one jumped in and said, *I do that exercise differently, and I think it works really well.* She then went on to explain how SHE does it.

— When someone asks your spouse or children a question, you answer for them.

— In a group setting, someone is recounting a rather dramatic incident, and then several others begin talking about an incident of their own that is even more dramatic. A real ego competition to determine who will be the most important when all is said and done.

The ego justifies itself and defends itself

> **In about 90% of the situations when we answer on the defensive, no one asked us for an explanation.**

The ego is convinced it must defend itself against everything and everyone. It readily shifts to the defensive. The ego thinks it's always someone else's fault and seeks to pin the blame on someone.

Here are a few examples to help you become more alert and cue into how many times we can be inclined to justify ourselves and seek out someone to pin the blame on.

— I was waiting in line at the airport in another country to go through customs. After a half-hour wait, I noticed I was standing in the wrong line – the one I was in was for residents. *Oh no! How come these things happen to ME? If they had put their signs in the right place, I wouldn't have ended up in the wrong line.*

— When you come in late, have you noticed you have already prepared your excuse even before arriving? You're even ready to lie to avoid getting caught. Every lie stems from the ego and is hiding one or several unconscious fears.

— You're discussing the country's economic situation with friends, but the others disagree with you. However, you go to great lengths to get them to agree and you add many reasons why your opinion is important and true. **You're not your opinion**. It's only your ego that thinks it is.

— *I can't trust men anymore. I've had three husbands and every one of them cheated on ME. They're the reason I am now alone.*

— *If only I had had parents who had taken better care of ME, I wouldn't be dealing with all of these problems today.*

— *MY poor back! It's that way because of a fall when I was 10.*

— *If you had been a better wife and felt like making love with ME more often, I never would have cheated on you.*

We are also on the defensive when we're criticized, caught off guard, when our opinion is questioned or someone tries to give us some advice. We feel under attack, and rarely is that ever the case.

— For example, I ask my husband to go to the supermarket for me, he comes back with what I asked him to get, and suddenly I say, *Dammit, I forgot to put onions on the list.* His ego takes over. He really didn't listen to what I said and retorts, *It's not my fault. I had no idea you wanted onions.*

— A couple returns home after spending the evening at their friends' place. He tells his wife how much he enjoyed the meal and that the apple pie, in particular, was good. Feeling singled out, his wife shoots back, *Are you telling me she makes better pies than ME? Or I've got more to do than make apple pies. She doesn't work.*

— You leave the cinema with your husband and he mentions that he didn't like the movie, and you were the one who insisted that he come along. *Why can't you agree with ME for a change? It's almost as if you take the opposite side on purpose just to tick me off. The movie was great – you're the one with no taste!*

— *Why is he telling ME how to do it? Does he think I'm a fool?*

The ego can't exist in the present

When you talk about or think about incidents in the past, or have regrets or dream about the future, hoping that things will get better than they are now, you're not centered and not in your heart. The ego strives to feel important over what has happened or what could happen in the future.

— *If only I had the energy I had when I was young, life would be better.*

— *If I hadn't lost MY job, everything would be different today.*

— *Wait until I get MY medical degree. You'll see. I'll be making big money and MY life will be different.*

— *When I'm finally able to take a vacation, I'll be able to rest, and I'm sure I'll reach MY goal when I get back.*

— *It's a shame the way we lose self-confidence when we age! Let me tell you that when I was young, nothing could stop ME. I had courage and confidence to burn!*

— *When I get back to MY normal weight, I'll finally be able to meet MY future spouse.*

— *I can hardly wait to retire! I'll finally be able to listen to MY needs.*

Since the ego is rooted in the past, it forces us to remember all of incidents in our past that caused us suffering.

Our ego hangs on to all of our traumas for years. The more important they become, the more the ego is convinced of its existence

---

The ego maintains that our suffering is caused by other people, and it urges us to dig up memories of difficult incidents. Unfortunately, it is only its PERCEPTION that turns us into victims following a trauma. I am not saying that there are no victims of evil acts in life. However, if we continue thinking about and running the same film in our head, we will be increasingly traumatized by the incident.

How many people lived through atrocities during wars or accidents, for example, and emerged stronger and more courageous? Everything depends on our ability to assume that everything we attract to ourselves is our own creation. I will get into this notion of responsibility later in the book.

The ego feeds off the notion of good and bad

Every time you think of something *good* or *bad*, those thoughts originate from your ego. It maintains that when you do something good according to the criteria it has learned, it is important and really does exist. When you do something it considers *bad*, it risks losing importance and therefore its identity. Your ego is convinced that when you don't listen what it believes is best for you, it's not worth listening to. It cannot fathom how you can have needs different from what it believes. That is why all of us live burdened with heavy guilt.

> ## The more you live with guilt, the more you are allowing your ego to run your life

When you are centered, you do not describe anything as being good or bad. You are simply aware that you are living an experience that may or may not be an intelligent one for you (according to its consequences). Your ego doesn't know you need all of these experiences to learn. When you're centered, there are no value judgments – only observation.

Here are a few more examples that include judgments of good or bad.

— *I lost my cool again with the kids. When am I finally going to learn to be more tolerant?*

— *I really didn't need that second piece of cake.*

— *I really did a good job! I hope this time my boss will be satisfied and will compliment ME!*

— *I hope MY husband will not notice that I haven't done the washing yet. He never realizes everything that I have to do. Even when he doesn't say anything, I can see it by the look on his face that he thinks I'm lazy if everything isn't perfect around here.*

— *When am I going to be able to think twice before I speak? I can see she didn't like what I just said, yet again.*

The ego makes comparisons

When you make comparisons involving yourself or others for better or worse, the ego is always the driving force.

— *How come I'm not as pretty as my sister? It's not fair.*

— *I may not have as many degrees as my work colleague, but MY love life is much better than hers.*

— *I don't understand why he doesn't want to listen to MY advice. It seems to ME he could follow it very easily.*

— *Life was far more straightforward in MY day.*

— *I've been working for this company for 20 years. Why are they more inclined to recognize newcomers for their ideas?*

If you're in the presence of people you think are more knowledgeable than you are, you don't know how to act, because your ego is telling you that if you do open your mouth, you will be monopolizing proceedings, or that you will be a laughing stock; and that if you don't talk, you'll look ignorant or bizarre.

The ego believes it's able to make other people happy

The following will probably surprise you – every time you worry for others, when you want to help them even though they didn't ask for help – it's an indication that your ego is taking over your life. It won't like that statement and will subtly tell you, *Don't believe a word of it. You know full well you are worried for loved ones because you're a good person and you are only looking out for their happiness.*

I agree that you're a good person if you are concerned about the happiness of people close to you. **The message I want to get across is that you're going about it the wrong way**. Your wanting to do everything for others rarely goes over well with them. They could even feel offended that you are sticking your nose into something that is none of your business by telling them what to do, when they haven't asked you for anything and when you yourself have problems to solve. They could even take it as a put-down when you don't think they are able to ask for help.

One of my sons is an inventor, a creative genius in my estimation. What excites him is the time he spends on a project. Problem is that he quickly changes his mind. Instead of marketing his inventions or bringing a project to fruition, as soon as a new idea comes along, it immediately captures his interest. He starts right from square one with no perspective. As an enterprising and daring woman who sees an idea through to the end, I found this kind of behaviour very hard to watch for the longest time. How many times did I say to myself, *How can he live like this at his age, with nothing to his name, starting over time and time again?*

For years, I criticized him and gave him all kinds of advice so that he could achieve success with his brilliant ideas. I even tried to help him by investing in two of his companies. Nothing came of it, as he had once again turned his attention to something else.

I came to the realization that my ego was behind my wanting him to succeed at all costs. My son's success would have flattered me. I wanted to help him to satisfy my ego. It was a lengthy process stretching over several years, and as I am writing this, my son still has not changed. He works on two different projects at the same time. I have decided to invest yet one more time to find out whether I could do it just out of my love for him and not for my own glorification. It was just to see whether he chooses to use my money in a way that doesn't please me, and it will also give me an opportunity to practice letting go.

I suggest that you proceed with caution whenever you worry about someone else. Every time you try to help without being asked to, you will discover you fear for yourself if that person does not follow your advice. Your ego is afraid, and it also believes it is becoming more important if the other person succeeds **thanks to the advice and the help you provided**.

Even when someone asks you for help, do you say yes unconditionally, or do you decide to help with the hope of gaining recognition when the person does succeed? The latter is conditional, and all it does is satisfy and feed your ego.

Arrogance

Our ego is never satisfied, and the more importance it acquires over time, the more it fears losing this importance and the more it seeks to gain. Our ego even manages to develop arrogance, which is also described as *having a big ego*. **Arrogance is ego at its apex**.

Arrogance is an exaggerated feeling of its own value, an overestimation of oneself that tends to place a person above others. Arrogant people want to win at all costs and to be right.

> **Our ego is always trying to impose its value system on us, and when it also tries to impose itself on other people, arrogance is the end result.**

Arrogant people think they are so important and powerful that they convince themselves that only they are the custodians of the truth, thereby believing they are better and superior. They try to convince others to believe in the same things they do – they want to dominate. They are specialists in finding many reasons to get others to believe them and act the way they want. Behaviours and attitudes that put down others give them a feeling of superiority. Striving to be right whatever the cost implies that others are wrong.

Here are a few examples of arrogance in action:

— *When are you going to stop smoking? You know it's not good for your health. I managed to stop, and so should you, just like I did.*

— *MY husband doesn't want to follow ME and take personal development courses. He is no longer at the same level as ME. I'm afraid it is affecting our relationship.*

— *How come you're not able to put everything away as you go like I do? Can't you see that is a smarter way of doing things?*

— *Don't you realize that your way of raising children is the wrong one? You are too permissive. You should try MY method. It gets far better results.*

— *It's your fault I'm mad – you're the one that started it.*

Arrogance can be manifested either intellectually or spiritually. An intellectual that is arrogant especially uses their knowledge to boost their standing. The impression produced by the way they speak about their knowledge could be something along the lines of, *Listen to me. I know better than you.* They often speak fast and their voices get louder when they realize they can't convince others.

The spiritually arrogant person believes they are superior in terms of their being. *I'M better organized than you. I'M more patient than you. I'VE evolved more than you have...* This can be readily sensed in what they say, even though they don't phrase it in these words.

I could cite thousands of examples where we try to convince someone else to act or to be like us. Our ego wants to have us believe we are acting for the good of other people. It also believes that the more importance it gains, the more power it has to scare people. Thus, it believes it will not be as afraid. This is but an illusion, because we all know that a big dog is often more fearful than a smaller one.

Have you ever noticed that a comment wrapped in arrogance does not produce any results? The more arrogant we are, the more other people put up resistance, because they feel put down and compared. Arrogant people seek to be powerful, which is only pleasing to their ego. The person being put down knows down deep that this attitude is the opposite to true love that accepts differences in others.

> ## An arrogant behaviour conceals a huge fear of being rejected and not being loved.

Someone acting in n arrogantly symbolizes someone who **is seriously lacking in self-confidence**. That is why they seek to compare themselves favourably to others. Their lack of seif-esteem means they cannot feel self-confident, pay themselves compliments, and even love themselves. That is where their **need for the outside** comes in, particularly their search for love and other people's approval in order to be happy.

Someone who adopts arrogant behaviours has embarked on an idealistic quest for perfection. An idealist is the opposite of a realist. Consequently, if you see yourself as someone who is rarely ever satisfied and who must start everything over and often review what you have done to ensure that it's perfect, it means your ego is terrified of being rejected.

Unfortunately, it is impossible for the ego to know that perfection only exists in a spiritual world, not in the material world, since the ego has absolutely no idea that the spiritual world even exists.

People who are too idealistic often compare themselves unfavourably with others or refuse to accept a compliment. Your ego will do all it can to convince you that admitting you are inferior will make you a humble person. Quite the opposite is true, because this is but one more trick the ego uses to gain the upper hand.

Let us take the example of Janine who is always putting herself down, because she thinks she is not a good cook. When guests come over, the first thing she says is: *I prepared an*

Italian dish for you, even though I know I don't cook as well as all of you do. I do hope, though, that you'll like it just the same.

When she makes comments like this, she is fishing for compliments from her guests who will try to reassure her. The unfortunate thing is that even though her guests will go out of their way to assure her everything is just great, she will not believe it and will begin the same refrain when the next available opportunity presents itself. She will never be satisfied with her culinary skills, because her ideal is unrealistic.

Did you ever wonder what the world would look like if all of our behaviours and attitudes were the same, if everyone believed in the same notion of good and bad? What a monotonous world it would be! Moreover, we would never have a chance to verify the extent of our true love and our ability to accept.

If you are the type that often throws in the towel, who doesn't stand up for yourself and believes that others are arrogant, I suggest that you look further than that. More often than not, someone who slinks away and allows others to walk over them is suppressing their own arrogance. They are only experiencing this on the inside to let nothing show by saying: *No sense fighting with him. There's no talking to him. I won't say anything, but I know I'm right. I'll just see to it that I'll do what I want to do anyway.*

With all of the examples provided in this chapter, I do hope you are more aware of the effect your ego has on your life. My intent is not to discourage you. All I want to do is to have you become aware of it.

> ## No change can be made for as long as you are not aware of what you want to change

As years go by, it becomes increasingly urgent and important to recognize the extent of the power we have given to our ego, not only in this life but also in many previous lives. The ego has realized since time immemorial that it has been instrumental in maintaining our fear of being wounded (the five wounds of the soul). Only when you develop your awareness one day will you be able to regain power over your life and allow the tremendous power you have within, which knows the needs of your soul, regain its rightful place.

In the following chapters, you will discover how you can gradually reduce the influence your ego has to set you on the path of becoming the master of your life. You will then be able to establish links between wounds and the various expressions of your ego which, I hope with all my heart, will help you to become yourself and stop using masks to protect yourself.

Now that I have read this chapter, this is what I have decided to apply to my life:

_____

_____

_____

_____

_____

_____

_____

_____

_____

_____

_____

_____

_____

_____

_____

_____

Chapter Four

Reducing the ego and wounds

How do we go about gradually scaling down the power of our ego? First of all, we must accept it and not be angry at ourselves for creating it. We must realize that, up until this point, humans have believed it was the best way of protecting themselves from suffering. The ego can be compared with a servant who tells his master what to do, because the latter has given him a great deal of power by authorizing him to do so.

Today, with awareness having been brought to the forefront, we now know that we are this master who realizes that having the servant decide is not a normal state of affairs. It must instead pay heed to its master's needs. We want to regain control of our life. With an attitude of acceptance, the ego does not feel it is being accused and believes instead it is being recognized for the help it tried to provide us in the past. It will be happy and relieved to resume its role as a servant and will gladly let us once again become our own master.

May we always bear in mind that we are not our ego, and let us reconnect with our divine essence. We are perfect beings who use a body of matter with its physical, emotional and mental dimensions to live certain experiences with a view to returning to our true nature and once again becoming a pure spirit. Unfortunately, we have forgotten this over time, and we thought we were doing the right thing by using our mental energy to create an ego for ourselves. Let us reconnect with our individuality and with who we really are.

If you are honest with yourself, you have certainly recognized yourself in some of the various examples illustrating how the ego goes about feeding itself and feeling it exists. However, it may also be true you are not aware of it when it prompts you to deny everything that concerns you and instead point the finger at other people's behaviours.

This is very commonplace, because every time we discuss ego and pride in our workshops, my teachers and I have noticed that many participants do not hear what we are saying or distort what they have heard.

Getting help from friends and family

As a first step in the process of helping you reduce your ego's influence, I suggest that you reread the preceding chapter and make note of the various expressions of your ego.

When you are TRULY willing to admit that it is encroaching quite a bit on your life, find someone who knows you well and is able to tell you the truth. Show that person the list and ask them for their opinion on the behaviours and attitudes they observed where your ego is present, which indicates that one of your wounds is active and that you have donned a mask. If they make a suggestion to add other behaviours you find hard to accept, be conscious of the fact that the resistance is coming from your ego.

Don't take it too hard. It's quite normal that you have trouble doing this exercise, because the ego does not want to hear that it can do anything that hurts you. It is so convinced it is right and intent on helping you it will do everything possible to keep you unaware of its power. If you listen to your heart, you'll breeze through the exercise.

To delve further into this exercise, you can ask this person or some family members or friends to point out to you when you use expressions such as the following:

— *Well, I for one...*

— *I know it or I knew it.*

— *I told you so*, without anyone asking you.

— *Yes, but...; No, but...*, which indicates justification.

— *Listen*, meaning: *I want you to listen to me, because I know I'm right.*

— *Do you know what I mean? Meaning: Do you finally understand that I'm right?*

— *I've moved on from that!!!*

The message sent by physical disorders

Your inner God also uses physical disorders to show you that the grip your ego has on you is causing you to suffer. All physical disorders tell us about the extent our soul is suffering when we lack self-esteem. The more intense the physical pain, the more urgent it becomes for you to clue into the fact there's a lack of love in all areas of your life.

When your body is beset by stiffness, a hardening of the joints and arteries, constipation, etc., these disorders are telling you the extent to which your ego wants to be right. This especially means that you must, for the time being, agree to have been so afraid of being wounded that you unconsciously allowed it to control you. This is neither good nor bad. Being afraid is simply part of the human condition.

To summarize then, when you find out the cause of a physical or psychological disorder, it doesn't mean that you did something wrong or that you have to change your behaviour or attitude to be well again. The main message is especially being glad that you became aware of it. Now you must allow yourself to be that way for the moment, knowing that down deep, you gradually want to become your own master once again.

Psychologically, you know you're ego has gained the upper hand as soon as you wear a mask associated with one of the wounds. You can therefore review all of the behaviours and attitudes associated with the wounds which are described in detail in Chapter one.

Accepting the ego

By accepting it in your current life, you will be more readily able to admit when you're wearing a mask and you are not listening to your heart. This acceptance is a proof of love, and only love can transform anything.

> **Loving yourself means giving yourself the right to be what you are for the time being. It's the only way for an inner and outer transformation to manifest itself.**

I wish to share an experience that I am living now as I am writing this. I am on a cruise, accompanied by one of my sisters, and I take advantage of the days out in the ocean to write a part of this book. Since my husband and I have already taken numerous cruises with this company, I learned prior to my departure that I was a five-star customer, which wound earn me numerous privileges.

I was very pleased about it, not realizing that I was also very flattered to be considered a "special customer." Each time I was entitled to a privilege, I made sure I received it by saying:

— *I received an invitation to this meal. I AM a five-star customer.*

— *I AM a five-star customer, and I'm told I can leave the ship first without having to wait in line.*

— *Have you forgotten to give me the 50% discount coming to me for this bottle of wine? I AM a five-star customer.*

— *I AM a five-star customer. I was told I have a free day at the spa. Is that right?*

And on it went for each privilege. When I was told: *Of course, madam. Welcome to our establishment, and it's nice to see our loyal customers.* My ego was satisfied and felt very special, which reinforced its idea of importance. It took several days for me to realize that the five stars had already been printed on my cabin card that I had to show the staff. There was no reason for me to constantly remind them of this.

As soon as I agreed that my ego had gained the upper hand, without criticizing or judging me, I was able to follow my heart. I simply accepted the generosity this company extended to me and I was grateful to them, without always having to say: *I AM a five-star customer, except when someone asked me.*

The ego glorifies itself with all material things. The heart is able to recognize its divine power and is simply grateful.

Pride and ego

You're perhaps wondering whether this means we should never be proud of our successes or accomplishments. That is not the message I'm trying to get across. Of course, it is important to be proud of yourself, because it bolsters your self-esteem and self-confidence. However, pride lives inside you. There is no need to shout this from the rooftops to receive recognition or compliments from others.

When we are very proud of ourselves for getting through an ordeal, reaching a goal or meeting a challenge, complete with the satisfaction of having summoned up the tremendous power deep down inside us, we have acted according to our heart. We don't even have to talk about it to other people. They will realize it on their own and will probably congratulate us. If that happens, all we have to say is thank you.

If you feel a need to share a great victory, make sure your intent is not to pump yourself up and be congratulated for what you did.

At *Listen to Your Body*, many people tell our teachers and me: *Thank you from the bottom of my heart. You saved my life.* I can assure you that this abundance of gratitude gives us an opportunity to display humility and just say *Thank you*, acknowledging that if a person turned their life around based on what we taught them, the credit lies with them because they went ahead and applied what they learned. We were merely the instrument they needed.

On the other hand, if after hearing a testimonial like that we go off and tell everyone within earshot that we saved the life of this one and that one, we would be giving ourselves a great deal of importance. Unfortunately, many caregivers fall into that trap and believe they're the ones healing their clients.

Dealing with other people's egos

You may feel resistance well up inside you when confronted by certain situations. Take the example of a man who loses patience with his wife and says: *It's not MY fault. MY wife is the one who gets me going because she has a very big ego. She always thinks she's right. If she were more loving and more able to admit that I'm right sometimes, I'd be different.*

It's true that not reacting is sometimes very difficult. One can even fly off the handle very frequently, only to regret afterwards what was said. So how do we deal with someone who always believes they're right?

My advice would be to act in the way that was described earlier when you discover your ego. The only way of getting a result is to accept the person's prideful behaviour. In reality, that person is fearful for themselves and feels wounded. Whatever the activated wound happens to be, prideful behaviour hides the fear of not being loved. Since this person does not love themselves enough, they are seeking to be loved by you and everyone around them.

Merely recognizing their fear and accepting it will help you feel far better. Not reacting and simply listening without saying anything may be enough for you. Bear in mind, though, that your ego will be champing at the bit to get the last word in and to be right. This will be a great exercise, which will perhaps be difficult at the beginning, but with practice, it'll become easier. We can even say calmly to the other person: *Can we just agree to disagree and each hold to our respective viewpoint?*

This method pays big dividends, and it will thus be easier for you to see that the other person is not out to hurt you or say that they don't like you. They simply want to be right to satisfy their ego, with the belief that it's the only way they can be someone important. In the last chapter, I will present other techniques that can be used.

Being taken advantage of

At times, we may feel that other people are taking advantage of us in various areas. For example, most of us have trouble accepting situations where someone has stolen our idea. This has surely happened to you. I often hear examples like this one: *My sister-in-law baked us an apple pie and said she was happy to have discovered the recipe. When I told her it was mine, she denied it.*

Personally, I remember the first time when a major injustice happened to me when I was working in sales. Since I've always been one to like to try out new things, this carried over to my professional life as well.

As soon as I came up with a new idea to present a product, I'd feel a great sense of pride, especially when it produced good results. I'd then share it with my boss. The following week at the general meeting, she announced she had a new idea and suggested that everyone use it. As I listened to her, I'd say to myself: *Surely she's going to thank ME and tell everyone I'm the one who talked to her about it. She never did.*

You can just imagine how angry I was! As soon as I worked up enough courage to confront her about it and ask her why she didn't acknowledge that I had shared the idea with her, she strongly denied having heard me speak about it before. I had every reason in the world to call her an exploiter, a liar, an ingrate, etc.

Incidents like these happened on several occasions, and every time, I not only held a grudge against her, but I also was mad at myself for being naive enough to be suckered yet one more time. I couldn't help myself. I was so enthusiastic about finding ways of improving my work that I'd just blurt out what I was up to, forgetting my promise to myself not to do so again.

My intent was never to prevent others from using by good ideas. All I wanted was to be recognized for them. I didn't know that my ego was after the recognition. If I had loved myself enough back then, I could have settled for just being proud of myself without absolutely having to receive public recognition. I have always continued sharing my ideas, gradually learning along the way that the joy I gained by discovering something new was reward enough.

The same holds for the *Listen to Your Body* teaching. Thousands of people use it, and I'm happy with the thought it can help them. Whether or not they know it comes from me is not important. I am not thinking in this particular instance that my ideas are being stolen.

I also know that I very often remember reading or hearing something in the past and using it, even though I cannot remember the exact source. In cases like that, I say to myself that someone out there could believe that I made off with their teachings without their consent, but I know deep down that my intent is only to help others and get the information out there. I too can acknowledge that others have the same intent that I do.

It is important to bear in mind that people don't take advantage of us. We're the ones who allow this to happen. When you accuse the other person, your ego is at work.

Personalizing your ego

Here's a suggestion I believe will prove helpful in reducing the grip of your ego and communicating with it. When you realize your ego is acting in place of your heart, personalize it and give it a name. Ever since I first applied this technique, I've found it so effective that I have decided to include in this book.

I named mine *Flyzy*. This is how it got started. Many years ago, I was attending a seminar out in California. One day, we had the afternoon off, and I was out for a stroll in the woods. I brought a pencil and a notebook to jot down some ideas on projects I wanted to meditate on during the trip. Suddenly a noisy fly appeared, swooping and darting around and around my head for several minutes. I tried to shoo it away with my hands and notebook. I yelled for it to leave me alone, but there was no stopping it. I couldn't soak in the nice weather and enjoy the natural surroundings. Several other minutes passed, and it dawned on me that maybe there was a reason why that fly came along.

As soon as I asked myself the question, I figured out that it probably wanted to draw my attention to all of the negative thoughts going through my head during my stroll. I was worrying about all of the possible consequences that would befall me if I did this or that. I also had angry thoughts about some situations that I had experienced leading up to that moment. As soon as I thanked my inner God for using this fly to help me realize that my thoughts were not coming from my heart, the fly disappeared immediately. That's why I decided to call my ego *Flyzy*. When my ego gets the better of me with its different little voices, I always get the impression I'm hearing bzzz.

In the pages ahead, I'll use that name when talking about my personal examples and the name *Canta* for more general examples. I would ask you to replace both of these names with names you've chosen to talk to your ego. That will get you used to talking to it.

Getting back to the example on the cruise ship, as soon as I became aware Flyzy took over and wanted attention, I told it, I know *Flyzy* that you enjoy that kind of recognition. *I know you want to help me by doing this, and I thank you. You can now go and get some rest.*

Talking with your ego

You talk to your ego because it simply adores the recognition! *Yeah, you say, but isn't there a risk that this increased recognition will spur it on to be even more powerful?* You'll realize on your own that the opposite is true when what you say carries a message of acceptance.

> **When you talk to your ego and recognize that it is acting with good intentions by wanting to help you, it will be pleased, not realizing that your acceptance helps reduce its effect.**

It is impossible for the ego to grasp the meaning of the word acceptance. It can only understand what is mental, whereas unconditional *acceptance* of a fact or a person comes from the heart. It is a spiritual notion, not a mental one.

I am reiterating here the definition of acceptance, as I do in every book, every workshop and every conference. Even though you've already read about it or heard it, your ego may well do all in its power to get you to forget about it, which is perfectly normal and human. The less importance your ego exerts on your life, the more you will remember the importance of accepting everything.

Accepting is saying yes. It is recognizing and observing without making any judgment as to whether something is good or bad. It is simply observing, even though we don't agree or don't understand because of our beliefs, of what we have learned in the past.

While reading this, you may end up thinking along these lines:

— *When I'm not in agreement, why should I agree?*

— *Come on now, I can't accept everything. Some things in life are downright unacceptable.*

— *If I act like that, people will take advantage of me. I will look weak, like a doormat that people can walk over.*

If such is the case, start practicing right now to talk with your ego. *I know, Canta, that you don't agree with the definition of the word ACCEPTANCE that I'm reading. I know you want to help me, but I'd ask you to let me read for now and not to worry. Before accepting, I will think about the consequences to find out whether I can take them on. THANKS for allowing me to do so, and I can assure you I can do so without your help.*

Every time you talk to your ego, it is very important that you do so, showing that you are aware of its good intentions and thanking it for wanting to help you. You must really FEEL its fear that you cannot survive without it getting involved. It is constantly afraid that you will relive one of the five wounds and that you will not be able to stand the suffering. That is why you must always reassure it with respect to the consequences of your decisions.

As soon as you accept and you follow your heart, this will illuminate the mask that is at play at that point with the light given off by your heart.

Remember you don't want to ELIMINATE your wounds. Instead, you want to ILLUMINATE them, heal them through acceptance.

The great thing about acceptance is that you regain your power by acting with your heart. You've stopped channelling energy to your ego, which diminishes its effect. However, since it is so happy over your accepting it, it doesn't know what is going on.

Remember that the more your ego diminishes, the more you are yourself. Only then can you heal both physically and psychologically from all the ills that reside within you.

Limiting yourself to beneficial beliefs and following your intuition

You have certainly noticed that whenever I talk about ego, I am referring to non-beneficial and non-intelligent beliefs. However, beliefs that do not embody notions of good and bad do benefit us as well. Keep in mind as well that a belief is good only if you are willing to change it when you discover a better one. For example, I believe in the reincarnation theory and the fact that we live several lives on Earth. However, if another theory came along that would help me feel even more that only divine justice exists, I'd be ready to subscribe to it.

By becoming ourselves more and more and by stopping our ego from running our life and consequently suffering less and less from our wounds, we WILL KNOW what is beneficial to us. *The less we believe and the more we know.*

> **Being oneself is knowing what we want by feeling what is beneficial to us, even though others do not approve of our choices.**

Knowledge comes from our intuition, i.e., our being when we are centered. Conversely, the ego thwarts intuition. You may often have trouble distinguishing *Canta's* voice from the voice of your intuition. Both are very subtle. The best way is to check on how you feel with what you are hearing from within.

Here is an example of what I experienced personally. I had just turned in when an inspiration suddenly came to me, a new idea for this book. I was just about to drop off to sleep and didn't want to get up to jot down the idea. I knew it came from my intuition, because I didn't perceive any malaise or fear. I was sure I wouldn't forget it. Suddenly, I noticed that I was repeating the idea in thought, I was drafting it in my head and I restarted several times. I then found out that *Flyzy* had just appeared. It was afraid I'd forget that idea and wanted me to be perfect. I told it, *Thanks Flyzy for wanting to be such a big help, but right now, I really need to sleep. I assure you that I'll remember it tomorrow.* As soon as I had finished, the fly took off, and I was able to fall asleep.

This is yet one more good reason for you to be more aware of each instance where your ego takes charge of your will. You will then be able to choose to recenter yourself, which will not only serve as a balm for your wounds and help them heal gradually, but it will also help you reconnect with your intuition to run your life in synch with the needs of your soul and your life plan.

Now that I have read this chapter, this is what I have decided to apply to my life:

_____

_____

_____

_____

_____

_____

_____

_____

_____

_____

_____

_____

_____

Chapter Five

The wounds of rejection and injustice

Before you begin reading this chapter, I would advise you once again to reread *Heal your wounds and find your true self*, particularly the chapters on the wounds of rejection and injustice. They contain numerous details and examples I have chosen not to repeat.

In this book, I have combined the discussion of both wounds into one chapter because of their interconnectedness. Both are aroused by the parent of the same sex as the child, or by anyone having played the role of this parent. Rejection is aroused at conception and the wound of injustice around the age of four.

A child suffering from rejection from birth believes that if they don't make any noise, stay out of people's way and always remain off to the side, they will be more loved and not rejected. A few years later, though, they feel increasingly rejected, because their family members even forget that they exist. They may then decide to lash out, prompting the development of the wound of injustice.

Some people suffer the wound of rejection all their life. Meanwhile, others are coping with a wound of injustice so pervasive that they end up convincing themselves they do not suffer from rejection.

A person whose wound of rejection is predominant, both in their attitude and physical appearance, suffer less from the wound of injustice that is less pronounced and more inactive. Every person has both wounds, even though one of the two is less apparent. One can readily spot which wound is dominant during a period of someone's life by observing their body and their behaviours when the wound is activated. Over the years, some changes may well be noted.

Let us consider the example of a boy who feels rejected by his father, because he preferred his daughter instead. When his wound of rejection is active, he says nothing and pretends he is not affected. He can also retreat to his room and immerse himself in reading, electronic games or some other activity.

Even though he holds a grudge against his father, he makes excuses for him and believes instead that he (the son) is to blame if his father does not recognize him as a person. He is striving so hard to earn the love of his parent that he cannot bring himself to believe that the father doesn't love him. The boy convinces himself that even though his father is strict, cold, indifferent, and even violent at times, he is surely acting this way out of love. That is called being *in denial*.

Some men who were beaten by their father have told me: *My father had reason to beat me. I knew he didn't want me to act a certain way, and I'd go ahead and do it anyway. He beat me because he loved me, and he wanted me to become a good person.* This type of reasoning is so typical of the wound of rejection. If the situation had activated the wound of injustice, the child would have lashed out and criticized his father for being unfair.

When a boy arrogantly lashes out against his father (or a daughter against her mother) and purposely does the opposite of what their parent would like them to do, the wound of injustice is at work. This can occur in young children or in a more obvious way in adolescence or in adulthood. The life plan of a child's soul determines prior to birth which wounds will have to be experienced the most so that they can heal gradually and thus help their soul evolve, and learn self-esteem.

When the wound of injustice is activated and observable in someone's behaviour, this does not mean the person is also suffering from rejection.

The wound of injustice helps us not feel the wound of rejection

The wound of rejection is **always** behind a wound of injustice. This is yet another tactic our ego uses to deny that we feel rejected. You certainly recall in the description of rejection, I mentioned that the *withdrawer* (someone suffering from rejection) is a specialist in denying reality, because that wound causes the most suffering.

Denial is a manifestation of the ego at its apex

Remember from the description of both wounds in Chapter one that the *withdrawer* and the rigi*d person* are very much perfectionists. However, their motivations are different.

Right from early childhood, their parent of the same sex would give them attention or compliment them when they did what the parent wanted them to do. That is why they push themselves so much and even go above and beyond, because they believe that nothing is ever good enough. The *withdrawer* wants to BE perfect to feel loved and accepted, while the *rigid person* wants to DO everything to perfection to feel loved. In both cases, they are terrified of criticism, but when someone feels rejected, criticism hurts them much more because it deeply affects their RIGHT TO BE. The *withdrawer* is convinced that any criticism of what they're "doing" is the same as being labelled "YOU'RE NO GOOD." That is why people affected by this wound are increasingly more fearful of being wrong as they age.

While writing this chapter, I thought about the many teachers who worked for *Listen to Your Body*. Those who, more often than not, were overcome by their wound of rejection while they were giving the training experienced far more emotions than those who were more affected by their wound of injustice. They had a very difficult time enduring criticisms from their inner withdrawer.

Feeling they were not up to the task of teaching professionals such as psychologists or doctors, they readily allowed the latter to bother them. They also had a hard time accepting criticism or resistance from participants. Their first reaction was to think, *I'm no good. I'm not a good facilitator. They may even fire me.* They were so afraid that they automatically attracted more criticism than those who were not affected by their withdrawing side while they were facilitating.

Those who forgot a detail or gave too many, thereby causing them to run out of time, would promise to be better the next time. Some even apologized to the participants, who never thought this was even an issue to start with. Their rigid side could later criticize them for what they did, and several even admitted to me they were afraid of getting a tongue-lashing from me if I found out.

I also noticed that these two wounds prevented them from readily accepting help from others and especially asking for help. The *rigid person* generally refuses for two reasons: one – they don't want to owe anyone anything and prefer to do without rather than having to return the favour another time, such as when someone offers to pick up the tab at a restaurant; and two – they're convinced the other person won't do as good a job and that they will have to redo everything. They often say to themselves, *I'd rather do it myself, because it'll be done to my liking, and besides, it takes too long to explain how I want the task to be done.*

The *withdrawer's* reaction is to refuse, thinking that they do not want to be a bother and that they can manage very well alone. They would feel useless if they accept help. When someone insists and they end up accepting, they think that refusing help is even more bothersome than accepting it. They do not want to bother other people, and they do not believe themselves to be important enough to deserve help.

Their deep and generally unconscious thoughts are along the lines of *It figures. He's offering me help because he thinks I can't manage on my own.* They cannot fathom that a person offering them help is generally doing so out of generosity and pleasure.

If the *withdrawer* finally accepts, their wound of injustice may take over. They will promise themselves to remember the help given to be able to return the favour and thus be fair.

In conclusion, the wound of rejection is always with respect to one's BEING. We judge ourselves to be a certain way or we are afraid of being judged. The wound of injustice affects what you HAVE or DO. We're afraid of having more or less than others, or doing poorly or too well. Fears of being criticized or found lacking are common to both wounds. To satisfy our wounds, we want everything to be fair and equitable. We must DO the right thing to BE acceptable.

The ego cannot understand that only divine justice exists and that the cause-to-effect dictum is always fair.

It is indeed impossible for the ego to grasp the concept of a divine law, because it only understand things of a mental nature. It can't know there is no use wanting to control the law of doing for others in return. This universal law is spiritual, highly intelligent and infallible. We always reap what we sow, whether or not we are aware of it.

When you are not affected by any wound, you will react naturally, as follows: *How nice of you to offer me help. I gladly accept.* You won't feel you owe someone else. In cases where you turn down help, check to see whether your refusal is a response to your need or whether you're afraid of something. Our ego affects us in such subtle ways that we must constantly be alert in order to be aware of it.

Remember that as soon as a wound is activated, you're no longer the one running your life. It's only the *little me of the ego* that is experiencing an emotion. As soon as you accuse others or yourself, you're no longer centered. You've allowed your ego to move in, think and act in your place. When you're centered and in your heart, you feel and observe what is happening, not engaging in mental activity, without the accusation that is always part of an emotion.

> # When one of the five wounds of the soul is causing you to suffer, you are not listening to your heart or to your needs.

Bear in mind the fact that the ego is doing everything in its power to prove itself and to have others know it exists. It is obvious the wound of rejection is worse for the ego, for this wound, more than anything else, causes it to think it does not have the right to exist and that it is nil.

In fact, I have concluded that the **prime wound of the ego is the wound of rejection**. The latter is always pressuring the ego to take over. It is then accompanied by and strengthened by the other wounds. The more wounds are activated at the same time, the more we suffer and the more the ego believes it is indispensable in protecting us. That is why it takes on new defensive behaviours, convinced that we will not be able to overcome so much suffering. It doesn't know that the more it resists and tries to help us, the longer the pain lingers.

That is also the reason why the wound of rejection is at the root of all major physical or psychological illnesses. The pain associated with rejection causes people to hate themselves and their parent of the same sex. They harbour a tremendous grudge against that parent for not having been a model who could have helped them exist and live in society. I remind you that you must first feel a lot of love to hate someone.

Hate has the power of triggering serious or even fatal illnesses and cause people to mutilate themselves. This emotion is sparked by a staggering inability to feel true love. It leads to one conclusion: the longer someone is steeped in hate, the greater the pain associated with this wound of rejection. I dealt with this in more detail in my previous book entitled *CANCER, a book of hope.*

Diet and weight

When it comes to diet, the wound of rejection prompts people not to gain weight. Generally speaking, most people who experience emotions are inclined to eat more. The *withdrawer* is the exception. They generally deprive themselves of food when they have accumulated a lot of self-hate and believe they don't deserve to be fed.

Since they have trouble feeling hunger, they often eat little. When they do go overboard, they do so with sweets that act the same way as alcohol – these substances help them escape into an imaginary world. When the *withdrawer* indulges in excesses, they can't put on weight. With their underlying psychological desire to disappear, they cannot create a body that is too noticeable. When they eat too much and when their wounds of injustice and rejection are both activated, they throw up the food to avoid getting fat.

When the wound of injustice is active, *rigid people* feel guilty, because their ego constantly tells them that they must have a nice body to be loved. The wound of injustice is behind any person's decision to follow a diet. We have seen that this wound prompts us to control ourselves the most in all areas. When both wounds are front and centre, the person can suffer from anorexia and throw up for several reasons.

When the wound of injustice affects how a person eats, they will gain weight mainly out of guilt. When they get to the point they lose self-control, they invariably feel guilty they are no longer able to control themselves. Consistent with their desire to have a perfect body and their belief that their excess weight will not be as visible, it will be uniformly distributed.

I explained the weight phenomenon in detail in my book entitled *Just listen to your body and eat: stop trying to control your weight.*

The activation of wounds

I remind you that all wounds can be activated in three ways. If you refer back to the triangle of life in Chapter one, you can see you reject yourself to the same extent you reject others and you feel rejected by them. The same can be said for all wounds. You will more than likely feel some resistance reading this, because most of us are more aware of experiencing a wound than the other two. I often witness this during our workshops, and I hear comments such as:

I REJECT MYSELF: *Personally speaking, I reject myself far more than I reject others. I am so self-effaced that it would be most unusual for others to feel rejected by me. Moreover, I don't really feel I am rejected by others. Quite the opposite is true. I feel they go out of their way to show me their love, but I'm the one that has trouble accepting it.*

OTHER PEOPLE REJECT ME: *I personally have always felt much more rejected by other people, and it started quite young with my mother, who made no bones about the fact she didn't love me. I was never mean like her, quite the opposite. I go out of my way to show others I love them. It is true I reject myself on occasion but never like my mother and other women in my life have done.*

I REJECT OTHER PEOPLE: *It is clear I reject other people much more than myself. In addition, other people don't react that way with me. It's as if the more they tried to draw me into their orbit, the more antisocial I become. I can't help it. I think of myself first and couldn't give a damn if it hurts others. I always thought it was self-love, but at the same time, I have noticed that I've had difficulty in my relationships. I come across as self-centered.*

It is normal and human to have these convictions, given the influence of the ego. The more we become aware of it, the more we realize how much power it has over us. If you see yourself in one of these examples, it is important to accept the fact that a wound is always experienced three ways to the same extent. By accepting this, even if you disagree, you increase your chances of realizing this more quickly when one of your wounds is activated.

Examples of wounds of rejection and injustice that have been activated

Here are a few examples of wounds of rejection and injustice, which includes the reactive attitude of someone wearing a mask. I emphasize that both wounds can be activated by anyone. When your wound of rejection has been activated, you judge yourself and come away thinking you're a dud or worthless. A tremendous fear is gnawing at you. When you angrily accuse yourself or accuse someone else who is the same sex as you are, the wound of injustice has been aroused. It will be explained how you experience the same situation differently, though you do feel it, without allowing the mask to gain the upper hand, which will provide a balm to heal the wound.

I do point out that when the wound of injustice has been activated, the *rigid person's* mask can be expressed in two different ways: compliance or rebellion. You're compliant when your body stiffens, your eyes become cold and stare unflinchingly at the other person. You don't say anything, but it is easy to sense the injustice you feel and the anger you're suppressing. Everything is happening inside you. This attitude can be considered as a transition between the mask of a *withdrawer* (rejection) and the mask of a *rigid person* (injustice).

Some remain confirmed *rigid people* all their lives. Rebellious *rigid people* defend themselves, yell and openly express their anger. They can often easily defy their parent of the same sex – and anyone who arouses the pain originally experienced with this parent.

In the following examples, when I mention the name *Canta*, remember to replace it with the name you chose to give to your ego when you speak to it. This can be expressed in two ways: either you hear it as a speech within, or it expresses itself through your words out loud. The more the wound hurts, the more we risk losing control.

How many times have we heard people say, *I'm sorry, I didn't mean to say that to you. I just couldn't help myself.* When we allow our ego to take over, it can even use our body to express itself, for example, through physical violence.

Let's assume you're in a group, and suddenly someone asks you for your opinion. You feel bad, you're not ready, you don't like being the centre of attraction; and you believe especially that they won't find what you have to say interesting and could even consider it as being false. You give a vague response and try to deflect the attention to someone else, or you find a reason to get up to go get some water or head to the washroom.

In reality, you're not the one deciding – it's your ego standing in and dictating how you'll react as follows, *Don't say anything. You know you're too dumb and what you could say is not interesting and perhaps even false. That way, you'll avoid feeling ridiculed and not measuring up. You'll suffer less by saying nothing. You know full well you suffered a great deal from being ridiculed or being ignored when you were younger.* By believing what your ego tells you, you put on your *withdrawal* mask and resort to reactional behaviours.

Furthermore, in this same situation, you could suffer the wound of rejection, while quickly becoming centered and observant quickly, rather than reacting with the *withdrawal* mask.

As soon as you would hear *Canta's* tiny voice attempting to tell you you're dumb, thereby activating your wound, you could take one or two deep breaths, drink some water if possible, and you then could say the following to your ego, I know you want to help me Canta, and it's true my opinion may not be accepted. *I know you want to shield me from suffering by telling me how to act. However, I do want you to know that, one day, I really want to love myself enough to regain my rightful place.*

I also want to know what it's like to feel good, even though others don't agree or even if I stumble around or make a mistake. I especially want to experiment that even though I don't know what to answer, it doesn't mean I'm dumb – only that I'm undecided for the time being.

I know your intentions are good by wanting to help me this way, but in fact, it is no longer helpful. I feel stronger now, and I believe I'm able to assume the consequences of taking my rightful place. Thanks for wanting to help me, but you can now rest and merely watch me as I venture to regain my place.

That is how you recenter yourself and begin to observe the activation of the wound of rejection. This approach means that the pain and fear associated with the wound will fade and disappear. You will not fall into the trap of wearing a mask and taking on all of the escape behaviours.

Did you ever think that, in situations such as this, if you don't say anything, some people may well come away feeling rejected and believing they are not important enough for you to bother answering them and taking part in the conversation? They may even stop talking to you or not even look at you. You, in turn, would feel they are rejecting you. That is a good example of the triangle in action. This is a case of you rejecting yourself, you rejecting others and you feeling rejected by them.

Canta will chime in with the following comment: *You can clearly see I was right in telling you to keep quiet. They are acting like you weren't even there. They're certainly saying that you are too dumb to take part in the conversation. So you're better off not attracting their attention, which will make things easier for you. You could even cook up an excuse to leave, as it wouldn't change things much in their eyes.* The choice is yours – either you continue believing in this line of reasoning, or you speak to *Canta* as shown earlier.

Let's now turn our attention to an example of an injustice. Let's assume you're a woman. Your mother is alone and, despite having been divorced for several years, never came to terms with it. She often plays the victim card to grab your attention by saying she's sick or turning to a never-ending litany of problems. She complains about everything: her physical problems, the weather, the neighbour, her ex who cheated on her, her lack of money, her children who don't come to see her often enough, and on and on it goes.

You're the only daughter, and your two brothers always have excuses why they can't see her. You take pity on her and, like a good daughter, you make it your duty to call her often and go see her at least once a week. When she starts complaining, you can't help yourself – you want to help her with ready-made solutions.

Unfortunately, she doesn't listen to you, and you become impatient. You find she is very unfair about not appreciating the efforts you go to. You even act rough at times, and finally you find a reason to leave as soon as possible. These visits have turned into drudgery for you, and every time you leave her house, you're choked up with emotion. When you behave in this way, *Canta* is controlling your behaviours.

If you were afraid of being unfair to your mother and decide not to go and see her anymore, *Canta* would have the following to say: *You've got to go see your mom. After all, you're her only daughter. You're mean when you lose your cool with her. You wouldn't want to be treated that way, now would you? You're insensitive when you show so little compassion for her suffering.*

If you determined it was your mother that was unfair with you, *Canta's* comments would be along the following lines: *Is she ever unfair! Can't she see you take time out to call her and visit her? In addition, she doesn't even ask how you're doing! All she does is talk about herself. For crying out loud, she's becoming increasingly self-centered over time. She doesn't even listen to what you're saying and interrupts you constantly. If at least she listened to some of your advice, her life would be so much more enjoyable.*

Can you see the extent to which your mother could be suffering from the injustice you are showing her in this situation? She would be suffering injustice shown to her by you to the same extent you would be unfair to yourself by feeling obligated to make your mother happy.

Since the wound of rejection is also activated when you suffer from injustice, *Canta* could have the following to say after one of your phone calls or visits: *Some daughter you are! You're not even able to be nice. Why can't you just keep your mouth shut and let her complain? You know that if you stop seeing her or looking after her, you'll regret it for the rest of your life. She won't love you anymore and may even decide never to want to see you again. Remember how you suffered when she ignored you for three months and didn't want to talk to you anymore.*

I'm sure your mother also feels quite rejected by your behaviours, especially when you come up with an excuse to leave quickly. Meanwhile, you feel rejected when she doesn't even ask what you're up to, as she is too wrapped up in talking about her problems.

These examples clearly illustrate the importance of having a dialogue with *Canta*. With greater awareness, you will be able to detect its comments faster and realize that it's the tiny voice of *Canta* you're hearing. You thought you were your own master, but that wasn't the case.

To get something to change, you could say this to your ego, *There you go again, Canta. You just won't get off my case, won't you? I know you have good intentions by telling me this and trying to sell me on what you believe. I know you're convinced you're helping me, but it doesn't help me the way you think. I'd like to remind you that I want to be able to give myself the right to be impatient at times and not always feeling like seeing my mother.*

I know you're afraid that I'll suffer, but I now want to take control of my life and learn to assume the consequences, if my mother didn't want to see me, for example. I simply cannot stand being manipulated by the fear of losing control and then feeling badly after. I suggest to you to take a rest for now, and you'll see for yourself that I can now run my own life and assume the consequences.

By gradually living the experience of being controlled by our ego and then managing to recenter, we find it increasingly easier to follow our heart. We learn to experience situations by observing them. After reacting for a few moments to the suffering caused by the wound, we can take a deep breath and say this : *I realize that this situation or this person has just awakened by wound of rejection and/or injustice. I acknowledge I'm human and that I still have wounds that need healing. For now, I feel rejected and/or I feel injustice. One day, I will get to the point that situations like this will be increasingly less hurtful.*

With this new way of managing your wounds, you observe what you experience and notice that it is neither good nor bad. It's simply human. Instead of judging yourself, criticizing yourself and judging others, you can allow yourself to still have wounds, like all human beings.

Before moving on to the next chapter, I suggest that you jot down over the next few days every time your wounds of rejection and injustice are activated and prompt you to wear your *withdrawer* and *rigid* masks. This will help you become more aware of what your ego is telling you. Also make note of what you decide to answer to it.

If you practice this continually, you will develop a reflex on how to dialogue with *Canta*. Do especially make sure to take the time to clearly differentiate between how you feel before and after your dialogue with *Canta* and thanking him. You will thus be truly able to experience the joy of being able to recenter yourself.

Now that I have read this chapter, this is what I have decided
to apply to my life:

_____

_____

_____

_____

_____

_____

_____

_____

_____

_____

_____

_____

_____

_____

_____

_____

Chapter Six

The wounds of abandonment and betrayal

As was the case with the wounds we described previously, the wounds of abandonment and betrayal are closely connected. Both were activated at a young age by the parent of the opposite sex or by anyone else who played the role of this parent. The wound of abandonment is activated between the ages of one and three and the wound of betrayal between two and four. I would suggest that you reread, if you haven't already done so, the two chapters dealing with these wounds in the first book on this topic before continuing to read what follows.

In the preceding chapter, I mentioned that the wound of rejection causes the most suffering and is more devastating than the other wounds. The wound of abandonment ranks second. The reason is because both wounds are held inside. It is especially characterized by crushing sadness felt in the depths of your being. How many times have I heard people say to me: *I feel so sad sometimes, and I have no idea why. It seems I have everything I need to be happy – a good relationship, a career, good children, and so on. Why does this sadness suddenly come over me? I feel it throughout my entire body.*

If you feel that kind of sadness inside, it's a signal that your wound of abandonment is more present than you think. It is quite possible you don't want to become conscious of it to avoid suffering and that you partake in a number of actions to convince yourself that everything is going well. Having an active social life is one example. However, when sadness can no longer be held at bay, it resurfaces at times.

When you realize it returns regularly, it means that it is time for you to learn to manage your wound of abandonment by accepting it and by taking action to help diminish it gradually. You need not resign yourself to it and believe that you have to live that way for the rest of your life.

The major difficulty confronting people suffering from abandonment is that their ego has them believe they never get enough attention and emotional nourishment. No matter what they do to get this, they are convinced they could and should receive more. They have so little love for themselves that they never stop looking for evidence of love from others.

This explains why someone affected by the wound of abandonment while they are eating can consume copious amounts of food without even realizing their body no longer needs any food. In this case, that person will not gain weight due to their psychological deficiency and their inner attitude along the lines of, *I am lacking love. I don't get enough proof that I am loved.*

I have already mentioned that when the wound of abandonment has been activated, the reaction is generally expressed passively. However, the reaction in response to betrayal is more expressive and stronger. Let's take the example of a little girl who feels abandoned by her dad who is not around very often. He is either spending more time with his son or his wife, or he's at work. She feels alone, she wants to snuggle up to him, get his attention, but she seems she never has enough even when he does give her attention and calls her *my little darling*.

She is much more attuned to what she is lacking than what she is getting. She often uses subtle ways of meeting her need for attention and support. If her father did not show her any affection or attention, her wound would be much more painful.

When she feels abandoned, she will cry in her room, feeling that she is not really loved. Even if she finds out how to get attention from others, she nonetheless feels profound sadness when it's not her father (or the man who has taken on the role of father) who fulfills her need for attention. When she has problems with her mother, she would like her father to take her side. If he doesn't, she not only feels rejected by her mother but also abandoned by her father.

She can also play the illness card to get what she wants. However, even when she does, her father may well make up excuses not to look after her. For example, he could say that moms are better able to look after a sick child or that he can't go to a hospital, because it makes him feel ill. In response, she may even move on to more serious illnesses. The poor little girl doesn't know she needs to look after the healing of her wound, and that's the only reason why she gets her father to act that way.

What activates this wound even more is when the child develops a major Oedipus complex. The little girl puts her father on a pedestal, whether or not he gives her all the attention she needs. She doesn't realize that her own lack of love is prompting her to look hard for love on the outside.

The wound of betrayal becomes active when she begins expressing anger, either in thought or verbally: *How can a dad who claims to love me act like that? Why does he call me his little darling when he never has enough time for me? Does he not realize how much I love him? I'd be so happy if he gave me more attention.*

She doesn't understand that he doesn't give her more attention even though she goes to great lengths to be nice and loved. She especially cannot figure out why there is such a difference between what he says, what he does and what she believes she is getting from him. She feels betrayed. From the time the unmet expectations cause anger to well up inside her, she begins to resort to more reactive behaviour.

If the little girl does not receive any marks of affection or attention, there is every likelihood that her feeling of revolt will surface more quickly. She will not understand why a dad who is supposed to love his child never shows it.

The controller shows their anger in two ways: they resort to sly methods to manipulate the other person, or they may do so in a more overt, forceful or clearly aggressive way. Some take turns using both, while others stick with one method more than the other.

In the earlier example, the little girl can slyly manipulate her father by lying to him, making promises to him she knows she can't keep, telling him what he wants to hear, while doing whatever she wants. She can become aggressive, throw tantrums, provoke her father into reacting, disobey him, be arrogant, accuse him of being self-centered and insensitive, avoid him, and so on. Her wound of betrayal is thus increasingly more obvious.

> **A controller opts for sly manipulation or aggressive manipulation to get what they want**

When she is an adult, she will have trouble trusting her partner. He will not understand how she can be very loving and dependant on him at times and suddenly do a 180 and become mean.

The wound of abandonment leads people to develop many ways of controlling the other while wearing the controller mask. They do this out of fear of abandonment. This fear is generally unconscious and, as a result, the controller believes they are very independent and do not admit they suffer from this fear. Their controlling behaviours help them avoid feeling the pain of their wound of abandonment.

> **They don't know they are doubling their suffering. Not only do they fear being abandoned, but they have also developed a fear of being betrayed.**

It was mentioned in Chapter one that women wearing the controller mask are noted by the shape of the hips and of the upper thighs being larger and stronger; and men by their strength and the size of the shoulders. This difference is because women have child bearing hips. Meanwhile, the broad shoulders and muscles in the man are designed to provide protection.

Their body seems to say to persons of the opposite sex: *Can you see that I'm strong and that I can protect you? With me, you won't have to worry about anything – I'll take care of you.* Even though this is what they are seeking to prove, their strength is perceived as control and a lack of confidence, not as protection.

In terms of diet, people affected by their wound of betrayal will gain weight due to the guilt they feel. It is triggered by the fear and guilt of not taking good enough care or by the desire not to take as good care of the other person, which may be a sign of weakness on their part. As a result, they will feel guilt over not tending to their dietary needs. Their excess weight will be centered mainly around the belly, hips and thighs in women and in the upper body in men. If the controlling man also wants to mother, he'll store the excess pounds around his gut.

I previously mentioned that we begin feeling the fear of abandonment and that the wound of betrayal gradually manifests itself. However, those whose life plan require them to resolve a more serious wound of abandonment will mostly adopt behaviours associated with that wound.

Their wound of betrayal exists, while being less present and obvious. They will experience it in a more subtle way. For example, they may encounter much difficulty sustaining a lasting loving relationship. They will find all kinds of faults with their partner, but they, meanwhile, will not be trusting.

Some may even make comments suggesting to others and to themselves that they are happier alone: *With a divorce rate of 50%, I've decided I've had enough. I don't want to meet anyone new. It's just too hard to find someone to have a good relationship with nowadays. I don't need anyone. I'm strong enough to look after my own needs.*

Every time we accuse someone of the opposite sex, the wound of betrayal is activated. Influenced by the wound of abandonment, we judge ourselves, we take pity on ourselves, and everything is experienced within. We find excuses and we look for other ways of getting the attention we are after. This explains why women—and men more often than you would think—endure violent relationships.

I have heard women tell me: *I admit that my husband beats me, but this only happens when he's had too much to drink and he can't control himself. He is really suffering, and I know he loves me. The next day, he is very nice, and he truly is sorry.*

Generally speaking, battered men don't want to admit it, and accurate statistics are hard to come by. Those who are unaware of their wound of abandonment cannot understand why someone can put up with this for years on end. Trying to understand resolves nothing. It is better to show compassion for all of these people who are suffering, and this will help you heal your own wound of abandonment, even if you cannot yet admit having one.

Believing that *pleasing* is synonymous with *loving* is another strong clue of these wounds in action. That is why *controlling* and *dependent* people have many expectations. The *dependent* person is convinced that if their partner always pleases them to the detriment of their own needs, it is a strong symbol of love. They even believe that jealousy and possessiveness are also manifestations of this. To prove their love, they will also give into the other person's demands without even determining what their own needs are, and will expect the same thing in return.

Meanwhile, the *controller* has the same hidden expectations as the *dependent*. However, the former will manipulate in a sneaky manner or by openly complaining or being aggressive. They will demand their partner please them; if not, they will create a scene, sulk, threaten, haggle or seduce. Their expectations are quite strong, and they don't realize that the strength of their reactions conceal their great fear of being abandoned.

For them, it's only normal for people to go out of their way to please them, and they always have good reasons to think of themselves before anyone else. If the *controller* shows a selfish temperament, they will be the first one to stick a selfish label on someone who says no to their demands.

It is impossible for the *controller* to admit their faults, since they always want to get the last word in. Their excuses are more in the form of accusations levelled at another person or a situation they are removed from. They are also known to lie easily to avoid admitting to their faults.

Control by the rigid person and the controller

The masks associated with the wounds of betrayal and injustice include a great deal of control, and I am often asked how to tell the two apart. The motivations and fears are what differentiate them.

To illustrate this difference, let's take the example of a couple who has been involved in an accident. The husband tells the family about it in the presence of his wife. *I was driving along at a reasonable speed, and out of the blue, a car came at us from the right-hand side. My wife, who was sitting beside me, didn't warn me fast enough that the driver didn't seem to see me. So she rammed into us. That's women for you. They're not made to be on the road!* Though he said this in jest, he was accusing his wife of not warning him of the danger and the other driver of not knowing how to drive. His wife got angry and replied: *That's just nonsense. The woman was coming out of a lane, and how was I to know she hadn't seen us? When I'm the one driving, I look in all directions.* She defends herself and justifies her position.

The situation aroused different fears in each of them. He feared that others would think he was a poor driver, when, in fact, he believes he's better than the others. With his *controller* mask on, he can't admit his faults, and he has to find a culprit at all costs.

His wife stood her ground and explained how she expected the driver to react. She was being influenced by the *rigid* mask. On the one hand, she judged the other woman by accusing her of not looking in all directions, and on the other hand, she is judging herself inside by not warning her husband in time. *Rigid* people often justify themselves out of the guilt they feel. They don't realize that if they didn't feel guilty, others would not saddle them with this guilt and would not accuse them.

The wife in the above example may also feel betrayed by her husband's reaction and when she takes on the attitude of a *controller*, she would answer something such as, *How come you are accusing others? Why can't you admit that you were the one driving and that it's up to you to watch what's going on around you? You're too proud to admit your faults, what else is new!* This is a classic case of two *controllers* squaring off.

Sadly, these kinds of attitudes stoke the ego and increase the suffering caused by the wounds.

The difference between controlling and asserting one's needs

It is very important to assert our needs, instead of waiting for others to guess what they are. Unfortunately, most people don't know how to go about it. The *dependent* and the *controller* are generally aware of their needs and are convinced they're expressing them very well, but such is not the case.

The *dependents* voice their needs in a complaint, with the hope the other person will guess what they really need. The mere fact the other person would understand their needs by telepathy would prove just how loved they are. The *controller* makes their demands in the form of orders. They expect the other person to understand immediately what they want and obey them to prove their love.

Let's look at a couple, for example. The husband comes back from work at different times every night. His wife wants to get across to him how difficult it is to prepare meals, not knowing what time he'll come in.

The *dependent* wife (in a plaintive tone). *I'm fed up eating cold or overcooked meals. I'd really appreciate it if you could call me to tell me what time you'll be in. You know I'm anxiously waiting for you to arrive, because I'd rather eat with you than eat by myself.* As you can see, she is only complaining and talking about herself. She is not formulating any clear and specific request. As a result, a situation like this cannot bring about a commitment from each of them.

The *controller* (in a strong voice): *How many times have I told you to call me when you're not coming home at the regular time for dinner? I'm asking you for the last time. I'm warning you. The next time you roll in late, you'll have to fix your own meal. I've had it up to here!* You can see that this isn't a real request –it's an order. Both of them have not come to any agreement.

A bona fide request would sound something like this: *I know it's really hard for you to let me know the nights you ex-pect to come in late. What I want to do is to prepare the meals with love, especially the ones that are your favourites, knowing that you will be there to share them with me. How do you feel about the idea that I eat alone when you are late for dinner and that when you do get in, you warm up your meal and put away your dishes? That will avoid me having to go through all of these emotions while I wait for you.* She must also take the time to listen to his needs in this situation. Then, together, they will be able to come to a clear and specific agreement on how to resolve this.

To be true

Rigid people and controllers have trouble understanding what TO BE TRUE means. According to the definition we use in our teaching of *Listen to Your Body*, being true means thinking, feeling, saying and doing the same thing. This does not force us to say everything we are thinking. When we are questioned about something, we must tell the truth based on what we think and what we feel. To be true to ourselves and others, we must also act in a way that is in keeping with what we say and do.

It is especially important to remember that when we are true, emotions and accusations are not part of the equation. We simply cite the facts or act based on what we are. At times when we speak the truth in our dealings with another person and they find it unpleasant, that person won't harbour a grudge. They will instead respect us for our courage and authenticity.

However, when we are being influenced by the wound of injustice or betrayal, we are operating under a false notion of what is true. We believe that saying everything that comes to mind without the other person asking us to is being true.

I remember acting this way many times with my first husband, when I wanted to straighten something out. I would organize an informal candlelight dinner, and thinking that I was truthful, I told him everything I was experiencing. Everything I was saying was solely intended to get him to change so that I would feel better. The *controlling* side of me gained the upper hand by allowing my ego to speak. I was not being true – I was only expressing my discontent.

The *rigid* person acts that way with someone of the same sex. They believe they are being true by levelling with the other, but in reality, they are judging the latter, accusing them of being unfair and wanting to change them.

Being true in a situation of discontent means being able to express what we think and feel, while checking to see how the other person feels as well. It is taking responsibility of our fears and desires. It is the willingness to find a solution suitable to both persons.

Examples of activated wounds of abandonment and betrayal

The following examples will illustrate the difference between behaviours influenced by the ego, i.e., when a person dons a mask, and their behaviours when they remain centered and in their heart. An explanation will be provided showing how someone in the same situation can feel a wound without allowing a mask to take over, which in essence equates to a healing balm.

When explaining how to speak to the ego, I will use the names *Canta and Flyzy* which I suggest you replace with the names you gave to yours.

Let's return to the example I described in Chapter three, when I spoke about what I experienced with my son. My wound of betrayal was activated every time I invested in one of his projects that he would abandon before it came to fruition. This wound is easy to spot, because you feel anger that is impossible to ignore, and you accuse the person of the opposite sex.

Having suffered so much, I promised myself every time that I'd stop helping him that way. I'd say to myself, *Even if he gets down on his knees and begs, I'm not going to budge. I'd rather be judged any which way, rather than place myself in a situation that brings me so much disappointment, anger and hurt.*

Time would go by, and there he'd be, embracing a new project that seemed so exciting and promising, and I'd say, *Why not? Maybe this time he's changed, and this time, he'll hang in there till the end.*

As you can see, my expectations were front and centre in these situations. I mentioned earlier that I had decided to help him in his current project, and my intention is different now. I realized long ago that my son is in my life to help me heal my wound of betrayal. I'll know that time has come the day I will no longer have any expectations of him.

That is not to say I am not hoping that his project will continue on this time, but I want to be able to feel good and not get angry if he were to announce to me one day that he was throwing in the towel yet one more time. Every investment I've made in his projects was MY on my own initiative. No one forced me into it. It's therefore up to me to take responsibility for my decision to help my son and support him in the pursuit of his dreams; however, this does not necessarily mean he'll succeed and meet my expectations.

It took several years for me to realize and to come to grips with the fact that these situations of betrayal were hurting me so badly because they were activating my wound of abandonment especially. Each time he made me a promise and then broke it, I not only felt betrayed, but I also felt he was abandoning me as a mom.

Because of my mask and my ego, I would say to myself, *Seems to me if he loved me just a smidgen, he'd try harder to stand by his word. He knows how that would please me. How can someone act like that with someone they love?*

You know what *Flyzy* was telling me, right? *I'd never act that way, especially with a mother who did so much to help him. What an ingrate! He's heartless!*

For me, loving unconditionally is recognizing that my son is the way he is. He flies from one project to the next. He's an inventor who is just gushing ideas, and he's always been that way. I know that everyone can, if they want, take on a different attitude at some point. However, you can't make a decision in someone else's place.

My son is suffering from a wound of betrayal as serious as mine, and as long as he does not accept the fact that he too is betraying me, nothing will change for him. Only he can do this. As far as I'm concerned, I must look after my own wound and admit that he has felt betrayed by my behaviours many times.

Listening to our heart is remembering the life triangle, which brings us back to our responsibility. By being responsible, I accept the fact that by investing once again, I run the risk that my hopes may not materialize, which will be one of the possible consequences of my decision. I will therefore not experience any emotions or feel any anger. I will not accuse my son, nor will I accuse myself of being naive for helping him, in spite of my promise to myself never to do so again. When I held it against myself in the past, I suffered from my own betrayal. I had not kept the promise made to myself, the same way my son had done.

This is how I answer *Flyzy* when it jumps in and causes me to doubt myself or my son. *What you're saying Flyzy is coming in loud and clear. I know you want to help me suffer less and that you disagree with my continuing to help him, in spite of all of the past disappointments. I want to thank you for helping me, and I acknowledge you have the best of intentions. On the other hand, I want to be able to help him without having any expectations and to especially learn to accept myself and to accept my son, even though things don't go down as I want. I want to learn to let go instead of wanting to control.*

I want to stay connected with my good intentions, not with the outcomes that will occur. Don't worry about me, as I'm able to deal with all of the consequences of my decision.

This experience taught me that the wound of betrayal conceals a major despair. That is why we try to control everything, with the belief that the control will bring us hope. Going forward, I know that I'll have more confidence in life by controlling less. Before, I lived with false hopes.

Here's another example of betrayal between a father and daughter, whom I will call Lucy. After saving up a considerable amount of money to pay for his daughter's university tuition, the father learned she was in love with an African. When she introduced her new boyfriend to her parents, the father was furious. He couldn't accept the fact that Lucy was going out with a man who, in his opinion, did not have much of a future in France. In spite of all his attempts to talk her out of it, she continued seeking him on the sly.

One day, Lucy announced to her father that she wanted to get married and settle in Africa. Her enraged father shot back, *If you marry that guy, you can bet that your mother and I won't be attending the wedding. Besides, I'll no longer consider you my daughter, and I won't want to ever see you again.*

Lucy did get married and went to live in Africa. I met her at Reunion Island twenty-five years after she left France. She never saw her parents again, and her three children have never met their grandparents. Lucy suffered terribly, but she wanted to stand her ground against her father who was dead set against giving in. This is a classic case of wounds of betrayal and a very powerful *controller mask.*

While attending the workshop dealing with wounds, she couldn't fathom how her father could have felt betrayed like her. However, every time a loving relationship is shattered by anger, this systematically points to a significant wound of betrayal. Only a *controller* can hang in there for the long haul, wanting to win at all costs and hoping that the other person will bend and make the first move to apologize.

When I asked Lucy: *How do you think your dad felt when his dear daughter, for whom he made many sacrifices to pay for an advanced education to set her on a path to a rewarding career, decided to chuck her degrees to follow her husband? How did he feel when his dear daughter, whom he hoped would marry someone who also would have been pursuing a fine career, didn't care a whit about what her father wanted and chose the opposite path? Can you imagine how he felt betrayed and unloved by you? Remember that a controller feels loved only when the other person responds to their expectations. They can't tell the difference between "please" and "love."*

Lucy began crying her eyes out. She was really able to feel that her father has been suffering as much as she has in the last 25 years. She suddenly remembered that her father had always been a racist. She never realized that she was unconsciously defying her father and testing the extent of his love by falling in love with a black man.

This is what Lucy should say to *Canta* when he comes on strong to convince her not to take the first steps, because it's her father's fault they are not seeing each other: *You know Canta, I've been hearing you repeat the same thing over and over for the past 25 years, and all the while, I've agreed with you. I know your intention is the right one and that you are convinced that if I never see my father again, it will put an end to my suffering once and for all. You're right. Maybe the steps I'll take to see him again will not live up to my expectations.*

However, I know I can't keep on going like this, because I'm suffering another way. I now realize that my father and I both have wounds of betrayal, and I want to experience what it's like to make peace with him. I'm ready to accept all of the consequences, so you don't have to worry about me. I only ask that you watch me and allow me to live this new experience. It's my turn – you've done enough all this time, and I wish to thank you for it.

Lucy also talked to me about the wounds of rejection and injustice she experienced in dealings with her mother. They both manage to speak over the phone a few times a year in secret. She would have liked her mother to take a stronger stand and insist to her husband that she wants to meet her grandchildren.

During our conversation, she was finally able to feel the pain felt by her mother, who is too afraid to confront her husband. Lucy herself also acknowledged she was afraid of her father's anger and that was why she wanted her mother to intervene. Since she was unable to, Lucy felt rejected and said to me, *I don't amount to much if my own mother is not even able to stand up for me. I'd never do that to my children.* Those comments came directly from her ego.

This is what Lucy must tell *Canta* when it tries to convince her of her worthlessness and prevent her from making peace with her mother, and instead continue to accuse her: *I get what you're telling me, Canta, and I know you want to protect me. Of course, I'd have preferred mom standing up for me and confronting my father. I now know that she can't do it, just as I have been unable to in the past 25 years. I want to be able to accept that fear in me and then be able to accept it in her as well.*

I know you disagree with what I'm saying, but ! can assure you I feel strong enough to face my parents in the future. I know your intention has always been to help me. But it's no longer of help to me, and I want to experience something else. Thank you for your help. You don't have to deal with this situation anymore.

When the workshop wrapped up, Lucy had set her mind to talking to her parents in the near future, especially to her father. She had decided to announce to them that she'd go and see them, that she couldn't stand the stonewalling any more.

A few years later, I saw Lucy during one of her visits to France. She was really happy that she had made peace with her parents, who wanted the situation to be resolved as much as she did but were unable to take the initial steps. Lucy no longer held it against her parents or herself. She felt a great deal of compassion in her heart, and the reunification went well.

How sad it was to have suffered for so long! We often wait until we get to our threshold of suffering before we take on a different attitude and follow our heart. Don't forget that **the first person who decides to take action and make peace with the other is the most intelligent one**. Intelligence is knowing that your happiness takes precedence over any fear.

The next example deals with betrayal and abandonment in the context of a relationship. A woman whom I will call Emily has been in several relationships, including two marriages. Each time she goes through a separation, she asks anyone who is willing to listen to her, *Why is it I seem to have a knack for attracting men who leave me when they discover that my personality is a bit too forceful for their taste?*

It is readily apparent her ego wants to convince her it is not her fault and that all of these men are weak. As a result, she experiences one abandonment after another, and due to her *controller* mask, she is quick to pin the blame on the men. *Canta* is the happiest in this particular situation, as it feels important and strong. This is what it's whispering in Emily's ear, *This is yet one more instance of your strength. You're head and shoulders above these poor slugs. When will they wake up? Are there any men around who measure up to you?*

Until such time as Emily takes responsibility and admits that the behaviours of her spouses are a reflection of herself, her relationships won't change. In order to get there, she'll have to take a different direction.

An excellent way of discovering what she doesn't accept from herself is for her to observe the behaviours of the men in her life, using the mirror technique explained in the last chapter. Judging from what she is saying, she definitely does not accept their weaknesses. When she admits to be weak herself without judging or criticizing, she'll be able to have compassion for a spouse. That's' how she will know that she really accepts this state of being in herself. Only through acceptance can we succeed in transforming ourselves and especially turn a difficult situation into a pleasant one.

You can just imagine what *Canta* says to Emily when a relationship ends with abandonment: *Do you see what's happening to you? Another relationship has ended the same way, because you didn't listen to me and went ahead and committed yourself yet again. Can't you get it through your head with all of these experiences behind you that men can't be trusted? They feel so much superior to women that they can't live with a strong person like you. Why don't you decide once and for all that you're better off alone and that you don't need a man in your life?*

Canta can't know what Emily's true needs are, i.e., learning to love herself and accepting herself in a romantic relationship. Her ego cannot know what Emily's life plan is all about. The ego only knows what's stored in its memory.

> ## The ego cannot live in the present – all it knows is the past. It keeps playing the same film over and over.

Here's what Emily must say to *Canta* when she launches into her speech, *I understand Canta that you believe all men are the same because of the experiences I've had. I know you're trying to convince me not to get involved in new relationships, because you want to protect me from the suffering that comes with abandonment. It's true that the suffering keeps getting worse. However, I know that I cannot come to terms with being alone for the rest of my life. I want to live another experience, to see what happens when I change the attitude I've had so far.*

To do so, I'm going to have to go off in a direction different from the one you think is best for me. I have learned that my history of painful relationships can be traced back to the fact that I have not allowed myself to be weak. I didn't understand this before, because I did everything in my power to show the entire world just how strong I am. Today, I have come to the realization that I am both strong and weak, and I have the right to be both. This will help me accept not only the strengths of the men I'll meet but also their weaknesses. I know you disagree with my decision, but I ask that you allow me to live my experience, because I'm strong enough to assume all of the consequences. You don't have to protect me anymore to shield me from suffering. I'd like to thank you for what you have done up until now. I know your intentions have always been sincere. All you have to do now is rest and watch me.

Gradually, by living the experience of being influenced by our ego and then successfully recentering ourselves, we have an easier time following our heart. We learn to live the types of situations described above by observing them. After reacting for a few seconds to the suffering caused by the wound, we can take a deep breath and say this, *I realize this situation or this person has just activated my wound of abandonment and/ or betrayal. I acknowledge the fact I'm human and that I still have wounds to heal. For the time being, I feel abandoned or betrayed. One day, I will get to the point that situations like this will hurt less and less.*

By managing your wounds in this way, you are observing what you are experiencing and note that it is neither good nor bad. It's simply human. Instead of judging yourself, criticizing yourself and judging others, you acknowledge that you still have wounds, like all human beings. It will thus be increasingly easier to discuss things with *Canta* and share what you are experiencing with others.

Before you continue, I suggest that you do the same thing as you did with the wounds in the preceding chapter. Over the course of a few days, make note of all the times you are wearing your *dependent* and *controller* masks, because your wounds of abandonment and betrayal have been activated. This will help you become more aware of what your ego is telling you.

Think also about writing down what you decided to respond to your ego. If you practice this continually, it will become increasingly easier to the point that discussions with your ego will become second nature. Especially take the time to clearly describe the difference between how you feel before and after you talked to *Canta* and thanked him. You will thus truly feel the happiness of having been able to recenter yourself.

Now that I have read this chapter, this is what I have decided to apply to my life:

_____

_____

_____

_____

_____

_____

_____

_____

_____

_____

_____

_____

_____

_____

_____

Chapter Seven

The wound of humiliation

Before you read this chapter, I suggest that you reread what I wrote about humiliation in *Heal your wounds and find your true self.*

The wound of humiliation is the only one that everyone doesn't have. You may well feel humiliated at times, but I remind you not to attach too much importance to the words. Don't confuse your feelings with the name of the wounds. For example, you can feel humiliated when, in fact, it's your wound of rejection that has been activated. Only by observing your reaction can you really determine which wound has been activated.

In cases where your physical being is not showing any characteristics of the wound of humiliation, I advise you to become aware of your behaviours in situations where you say you are being humiliated. This will then help you verify what you are feeling deep down.

The same applies to all the wounds. Many people claim they feel rejected or abandoned, but they react with behaviours related to the wounds of injustice or betrayal. They can become more aware of what is happening inside them, if they begin by admitting what wound produces the greatest suffering in a situation. It is then easier to admit that this suffering was shielding rejection or abandonment.

I repeat that it is important to determine which wound has been activated, judging by the behaviour that ensues. For example, if a girl feels humiliated by her mother, this does not necessarily mean this situation has activated the wound of humiliation. What she has experienced as humiliation may have activated the wound of rejection or injustice. Her reaction will determine what wound has been affected.

> **Only by truly accepting what you really are can each wound gradually diminish.**

For example, if you think you are working on the wound of humiliation when another wound is causing you to suffer, it will take you longer and be harder for you to accept who you are. Total acceptance is the only way you can heal your wounds.

To summarize the description provided in Chapter one, the wound of humiliation affects your relationship with yourself, not with others. I have observed that, in cases where someone is experiencing a situation affected by that wound, they do not try to humiliate anyone else. To the contrary, they try to defend or excuse the other person.

However, it often happens that others can feel humiliated by the behaviour of a masochist. Many people have told me they were ashamed of a parent because of their weight or their sexuality-related behaviours but their feeling could have triggered any wound, not necessarily the wound of humiliation.

All of our wounds are with us at birth. Their importance is determined by the evolution of our soul and the dominance of our ego. In conclusion, life starts anew continually, and since we do not remember our previous lives, it is difficult to determine how far we have evolved. Only by living experiences can we become aware of what we have left to do in the present.

People suffering from humiliation, believing they are be-ing watched by a superior power, very often feel guilty. Why? Because in order to heal this wound, they must give them-selves the right to use, and especially enjoy, their five senses. That is why behind this wound lurks a very sensual person who wants to take advantage of their senses while accepting and loving themselves. Since their ego is convinced it is not good, not spiritual, they face a major dilemma.

The major physical characteristic of a masochist is the roundness of their body, whether they are big or small. A round person who gains weight will be increasingly rounder. People suffering from a significant wound of humiliation have a body larger than the average, even at a very young age. More often than not, they believe they allow themselves to be as sensual as they want to be, because they dress provocative-ly and seductively, they eat a lot and they have a very active sex life. They say they like themselves that way and that they accept their weight. But down deep, they feel guilty about lik-ing physical sensations too much, especially vis-a-vis GOD, the supreme authority.

That explains why the wound of humiliation is experienced more with oneself. For example, if someone makes a dispara-ging remark about a masochist on how they dress, eat or about their weight, they won't hold it against that person. However, they may blush about it, poke fun at themselves, be upset with themselves for being like that and agree with the remark made about them. Judgments they make about themselves will be motivated by shame.

If they have it in for the other person, this means that another wound has been activated at the same time. If the wound of injustice is at issue, they will justify themselves or think it isn't fair and that they would never make a crack like this to that person. If the wound of betrayal is active, they may say, *So, do you think you're perfect?* before going on to point out the other person's imperfections. The wound of abandonment will prompt them to cry or complain inside, and if the wound of rejection has been affected, they will pretend not to have been affected, as if they had heard nothing, or they will just leave the area.

Being a spiritual person

The most important thing for persons suffering the wound of humiliation is their relationship with GOD, the supreme power. Fundamentally spiritual persons want to be worthy of GOD. They feel HE is always watching over them. They feel they are being monitored, whatever they happen to be doing or thinking. They believe they are never spiritual enough. I point out that a relationship with GOD has nothing to do with religion and can be experienced by people who are not practicing. The fear of a divine authority comes from unresolved situations in one or several previous lives.

If you recognize yourself in these descriptions, it is strongly suggested that you change your definition of what a spiritual person is. Always wanting to be dignified, generous and accommodating leads to the development of the ego. Instead of continuing down that road, bear in mind that serving others is not necessarily the path you should take to be worthy of GOD. The reason is that GOD only wants you to be happy, and the masochistic side of you causes you to put other people's needs ahead of your own, to your detriment.

I know this isn't easy, because you are probably used to the praise you get from people you help. They meanwhile ask themselves at the same time when you'll begin looking after yourself.

> **A masochist receives a lot of praise from the people around them. They believe they're hearing the voice of GOD who is blessing them, who is glorifying them.**

Being worthy of GOD is an invention of the ego. Remember that GOD is a creative energy and not a person who is watching you and defining what is good or bad. The notion of good and bad is nothing more than a human invention and is in no way divine. In reality, what you learn from experience is all that matters.

Your inner GOD wants you to recognize your tremendous capacity to create what is more intelligent for you, and you to recognize all of GOD's expressions on this issue. In addition, believing that you know what is best for others only serves to boost your ego. No one is born to fix other people's lives. When you want to help someone, do so only if that person has asked for help. If you do decide to help, do so not only for love of the other person but especially out of love for yourself, not forgetting your needs, and for what you can learn through this experience.

The fear of being free and serving others

Since being free is a masochist's greatest fear, they do all they can to be occupied by helping out their friends and family.

On the one hand, if they don't, they'll feel guilt. On the other hand, this will make sure they won't be free.

The attitude whereby someone believes they are indispensable to others is harmful, because it encourages the ego to develop and feel it is very important. A person suffering from the wound of humiliation generally seems to be humble and discreet, but they are effectively hiding their feeling of superiority over others. They often come away giving the impression they are infantilizing the people they're helping by wanting to do everything for them.

Since they are often tied up in resolving the problems of people close to them, masochists often don't have enough time to cook for themselves, but they do find time for others. They make sure they have something to snack on and will eat anything when they have a few moments. Given that they feel guilty every time, they continue putting on weight.

It is also quite common for a masochist to think about not eating excessively and opting to eat smaller portions frequently rather than a complete meal. In essence, they are saying to themselves and to others: *I don't understand why I continue to put on weight when I don't feel I eat more than other people do.* However, they know deep down that they are paying as little attention to their nutritional requirements as they are to their other needs, both physical and psychological.

They can readily guess what other people think of their body from the way others look at them. They then feel humiliated and are even more angry with themselves. Other people are only around to confirm what they think of themselves.

If these situations seem familiar to you, pay attention to how many times *Canta* speaks to you, as this can take place several times a day. Also take the time to respond to your ego, as explained earlier in this book.

When your guilt shows through following an excess relating to your physical senses, whether it is food, sex or any other abuse of the senses, tell *Canta* the following, *I know Canta that I abused my senses. You're right, but I remind you that I tried too hard to control myself before. I'm a sensual person, and my goal in this life is to learn how to manage my senses, while meeting my needs at the same time.*

I'm not there yet, and there are bound to be more circumstances where I'll go overboard, but I'd ask that you let me learn for myself how to reach my goal. I know some of the consequences may be unpleasant, but I feel able to accept them. You can now take a rest and allow me to take charge of my life now. However, I do want to thank you for all the help you've tried to give me. I now want to help myself.

The slowness of masochists

It often happens that people suffering from humiliation think they are too slow, especially when walking or running, for example.

Some have admitted to me that it was their way, often an unconscious one, of giving themselves more time to enjoy their senses. They must therefore allow themselves to go this route until the day they discover that it is sometimes good to take one's time and that sometimes, there is no need to do this to take advantage of a good moment. If this describes you, all you have to do to accept yourself is to set aside more time and use your organizational skills, a quality that you certainly must have. Remember that your time belongs to you and that only you can decide how you want to use it.

Example of an activated wound of humiliation

The following is an example of a behaviour influenced by the ego, when the person dons their mask and followed by the behaviour by that same person when they are centered in their heart. An explanation will be provided on how someone, confronted by this same situation, can feel a wound, without allowing the mask to gain the upper hand, which provides them with a healing balm.

Let's turn our attention to an example involving Monique, who has been married to Alan, a charmer, for several years. They have many friends and a very active social life. When they are entertaining friends, Alan always pays a lot of attention to the women who are present and has no qualms about putting his arm around them and wooing them in front of Monique. He believes his attitude is acceptable, since he is not hiding his seductive side from his wife. She pretends this doesn't bother her and says something along the lines of: *I'd rather have him act that way when I'm around instead of behind my back. At least, I know what I'm dealing with!*

Nonetheless, after one of these get-togethers, she told me that she would have liked her husband to dance with her at least once. When she brought this up to him, he shot back: *I don't want to dance with you, because you're too fat. If you want to dance, you'd better slim down.*

I can just imagine how women reading this will react. Talk about indignant. That's exactly what Monique felt. She was quite peeved, but she could see that her weight was an issue which ruled out dancing with her husband, as he liked slimmer women.

Her husband's attitude could have triggered other wounds aside from humiliation. In her case, Monique knows her masochist mask took over with the comments that *Canta* fed to her: *He's right, I'm too fat. I'm lucky just the same he wants to accompany me to these outings. I bet other women are wondering what he's doing with me. They must suspect that he doesn't want to make love to me anymore. He's right about finding me disgusting. I deserve it. I have no will power, I eat too much and my sweet tooth is my downfall.*

I often tell myself that I should slim down, but I just can't do it. On the one hand, I know that when I was slimmer, I was too sensual and many men found me quite attractive. But now that I'm married, at least my size helps me remain faithful to my husband. It's so hard deciding what I want. Being fat helps me control my sex life, but at the same time, everyone including me finds my body disgusting.

If you see yourself in this situation, this is what you could say in response to the little voice that is haunting you and causing you to suffer rather than continuing to keep it going and believe it: *Here you are again Canta. I know you want to help me by telling me it is normal for me not to be desirable with this extra weight. However, even if it's true that I do want to reduce, I do want to experience what it's like to feel beautiful and experiment with a fulfilling sex life with extra weight. As for my husband, he mirrors what I think about myself. I know when I allow myself to be sensual, he'll be attracted to me. You certainly believe that if I allow myself to be sensual, I could go overboard.*

I'll have you know that I feel I'm able to live with my current weight, and I'm willing to assume the consequences of being both overweight and more sensual. I'm asking you to stop worrying about me, and I thank you for trying to help me all of these years. The time has come for me to take charge of my life.

By living the experience of being influenced by our ego and then recentering ourselves, we gradually find it easier to listen to our heart. We learn to live with the situations described above by observing them. After a few minutes of reacting to the suffering caused by the wound, we can take a deep breath and say: *I realize this situation or this person has just activated my wound of humiliation. I am allowing myself to be human and admit that I still have wounds to heal. For the time being, I feel humiliated. One of these days, I'll get to the point that situations like these will hurt me less and less.*

This way of managing the wound indicates that you are observing what you're living, that it is neither good nor bad – it's simply human. Instead of judging and criticizing yourself, you come to grips with the fact you still have wounds, which is a major expression of self-love.

Before you move on to the next chapter, I suggest that you do the same thing you did for the previous two chapters – take some time out over the next few days and write down every instance your wound of humiliation has been activated and has prompted you to don your masochist mask. This will help you become more aware of what your ego is saying to you.

Then write down what you decided to say to it in response. With continuous practice, you'll find it increasingly easier to the point that your reflex will be to take matters up with your ego. Especially take the time to jot down the difference between how you felt before and after you hashed things out with your ego and offered it your thanks. You'll really feel the happiness of having been able to recenter yourself.

Now that I have read this chapter, this is what I have decided to apply to my life:

_____

_____

_____

_____

_____

_____

_____

_____

_____

_____

_____

_____

_____

_____

_____

Chapter Eight

Knowing which wound
has been activated

This is a question that is often asked by those interested in their wounds. I have already mentioned that knowing exactly which wound is at issue when you're experiencing a difficulty significantly increases the chances of resolving it more quickly. However, knowing which is which is not always obvious, and it requires practice, because we don't simply become an expert in a subject merely through knowledge. The only way is to experiment what we have learned or a technique repeatedly for it to become second nature.

For example, if you have already learned how to dance the cha-cha, merely learning the basic steps does not mean you'll be able to dance it easily. You have to practice the steps several times to the point you no longer have to think about it. As soon as you hear the rhythm, your legs seem to dance to the tune on their own.

The same goes for recognizing wounds. The best way is to learn to apply a technique. By going through the following steps, you'll ask yourself a few questions while you explore the problem.

Step one: recognizing your ego

Based on the information in Chapter three, you will easily recognize when your ego has taken over. By remembering that as soon as you have judged or accused someone else, that you think back in the past or in the future while feeling uneasiness, be it fear, worry, guilt, apprehension, indecision, doubt, anger, to name a few, you know that it has taken control.

For example, while I'm writing this book, work is being done on my house. I feel a sense of happiness that my surround-ings will be so nice, pleasant and comfortable once the work is complete. I am myself – I'm listening to my need for beauty. Since there is no uneasiness, I know my ego is not involved.

However, if I were getting into renovations to impress others and expect praise from them, that would be a clue that I was looking for recognition. The ego believes it IS the house, property, money, knowledge – in short, all material possessions a person can own. The more it identifies with these things, the more fearful it is of running short.

While the work is going on, I could be afraid of running out of money, being cheated by the workers or questioning whether this was the right decision. All of these examples would show me that this project is giving me more discomfort than joy, which of course could be traced back to the thoughts prompted by my ego.

In short, if you are unsure whether your ego is involved, ask yourself: *Am I at peace, happy and satisfied with this situation? Or do I feel some discomfort?*

ATTENTION: There's a difference between the activity of the ego and mental activity. You may have many things to plan and may have to think a great deal and reflect. At some point, you may feel mentally overloaded and need a rest. if you are not feeling any fear or discomfort within, you are merely observing a fact. In cases like that, you're better off doing something that requires no mental effort. Personally, I love cooking up a new recipe or reading an adventure novel.

Step two: discovering the emotions felt

The questioning continues:

— *What do I feel in this situation?*

— *Where are these emotions in my body?*

— *What am I afraid of personally?*

You cannot begin to heal discomfort if you are not even aware you feel this discomfort.

From experience, I know that most people struggle to answer these questions. People who have learned to feel what is happening inside them are few and far between. Most parents have not been able to impart this skill in their children, because they didn't know how to do this for themselves.

The following is a list from the *Discover and trust your inner feelings* workshop offered by the *Listen to Your Body* school. It will help you discover how you feel.

I suggest you read it slowly when you want to discover emotions that are felt in a situation of suffering. The more you find, the deeper you will delve into yourself and the greater your chances of healing. If you practice this exercise regularly, you will be able to find answers more readily without having to refer to the list.

Agitated	Aggressive	Amazed
Ambivalent	Angry	Annoyed
Arrogant	Anxious	Appalled
At ease	Ashamed	Astonished
Bitter	Calm	Compassionate
Concerned	Confident	Confused
Contrite	Crushed	Curious
Defensive	Delighted	Demoralized
Depressed	Desperate	Detached
Determined	Detestable	Disappointed
Disconnected	Disgusted	Disheartened
Dismayed	Disoriented	Distrustful
Doubtful	Dynamic	Edgy
Embarrassed	Energetic	Enthusiast
Envious	Euphoric	Evasive
Exasperated	Excited	Exhausted
Fearful	Feeble	Flattered
Free	Frightened	Frustrated
Furious	Glad	Grateful
Guilty	Happy	Hollowed
Hopeful	Hostile	Horrified
Hurried	Hurt	Idiot
Impatient	Impressed	Imprisoned
Incompetent	Incredulous	Indecisive
Indifferent	Innocent	Insecure
Insouciant	Interested	Jealous
Lazy	Lonely	Miserable

Modest	Negative	Nervous
Offended	Oppressed	Optimistic
Overwhelmed	Passionate	Peaceful
Perplexed	Pleased	Positive
Possessive	Preoccupied	Prudent
Relieved	Restless	Rested
Romantic	Sad	Satisfied
Scared	Sentimental	Shocked
Shy	Sorry	Strong
Stubborn	Stuck	Stupefied
Stupid	Submissive	Surprised
Suspicious	Tensed	Terrified
Thoughtful	Tired	Tormented
Troubled	Uncertain	Unhappy
Unjust	Unfair	Upset
Useless	Vulnerable	Wary
Weak	Withdrawn	Worn out
Worried	Worthless	Wounded

The following feelings are reactions to someone else and conceal a more deeply rooted feeling:

Abandoned	Abused	Accused
Acknowledged	Affected	Attacked
Belittled	Betrayed	Blamed
Cheated	Comforted	Contented

Crushed	Depreciated	Desired
Despised	Detested	Diminished
Dirty	Disclaimed	Dominated
Driven back	Dropped	Moved aside
Excluded	Harassed	Humiliated
Ignored	Insulted	Intimidated
Invaded	Irritated	Judged
Manipulated	Mistreated	Misunderstood
Neglected	Nourished	Offended
Protected	Pushed back	Rejected
Ridiculed	Secured	Stifled
Stolen	Trapped	Threatened
Used	Violated	welcomed

Determining what emotions you feel will enable you to easily discover what you are personally afraid of.

> **We never fear for others. We think we are afraid of what could happen to them, but in fact, we are afraid of the repercussions this would have on ourselves.**

It is important to be aware that fear belongs to your ego, not to your true being, except for an actual fear that is necessary when dealing with a danger that is present. If you can't find what you are afraid of, don't insist, just let go for now.

The following days, you can ask yourself the question a few times. *What am I afraid of personally in this situation?* If the answer is not immediately forthcoming, it means you're not ready to receive it. In that case, I suggest that you not force the issue. Ask instead your inner GOD to help you, and more than likely, the answer will come to you right off the bat either the next day or a few days later. Often, it comes through in the form of questioning: *Could it be that I'm afraid of...?* And there's your answer.

Step three: judgments, accusations, reactions

— *Who am I judging or accusing in this particular situation?*

When you judge yourself especially out of fear, the reaction to the wound of rejection and/or abandonment is the culprit. When you judge yourself out of shame, it is a reaction to the wound of humiliation.

When you accuse a member of the opposite sex out of anger, the wound of betrayal is at issue, and you're wearing the *controller* mask. You can either vent your reaction of anger or revolt or hold it inside. However, even if you're holding it in and are in the midst of planning revenge or you defer a confrontation until later, the pain you feel is just as intense. Holding it in creates more inner suffering and the problem usually grows, the longer you take to get it out.

When you accuse yourself or someone of the same sex out of anger, the wound of injustice has been aroused, and the *rigid* mask is controlling you. You react visibly by either justifying yourself or accusing the other person. Your reaction may appear quite obvious from the get-go, or you may hold back with the intention of letting loose later. Even if you hold it back, it is readily visible in your gestures, look and body language which reflect the anger you're holding back.

Determining who the accusation and the judgment have been levelled against will help you the most in finding which wound has been activated. Then it's the behaviour you use to protect yourself from this wound that will help you discover the mask that is in place. In addition to reading and rereading this list of what you feel, you should read several times the behaviours and attitudes described in Chapter one and the additional explanations in Chapters 5, 6 and 7.

Do not confuse judgment with the wound

I reiterate the fact that differentiating the judgment from the wound is crucial in determining what mask you are wearing.

Let's look at the example of Renee who is having a hard time with her boss. He ignores her and doesn't even look at her when he speaks to her. He clearly seems to prefer her colleague who is quite pretty. The working environment is becoming increasingly more emotional for Renee, and she brings this home with her. She cannot stop thinking about everything that is going on and *Canta* is invading her mind.

— *I don't understand why he's treating ME that way, after all I've done for him.*

— *Why does he only give compliments to Suzanne, when I'm the one who helps her do her work? Why doesn't Suzanne tell him I'm the one who deserves the compliments? She even has the gall to accept the praise with a big smile. What a hypocrite! And to top it off, she often tells ME she's lucky to have ME as a colleague. I know she's telling ME that just so she can continue receiving MY help.*

— *In addition, I'm the one who has to stay longer when something urgent has to be done. He doesn't seem to even think to ask Suzanne to work overtime.*

— *Today took the cake! He even had the nerve to tell me, "Renee, you look great today," as he examined me from head to foot. They both looked at each other with a derisive smirk. I'd rather he say nothing than hear stuff like that. The compliment really doesn't make up for all the other days I've worked with him for the past two years.*

— *I think I'm going to leave this job. I'm fed up being humiliated and rejected like that.*

Renee could easily conclude these situations are arousing her wound of humiliation. Although she finds this situation humiliating, other wounds are being activated.

Let's start with her boss. Since she does not react to him and keeps everything inside, his behaviours are activating her wound of rejection especially, and she is wearing her *withdrawer* mask. She withdraws and pulls away. She may well be unaware of the judgments she's been harbouring deep down inside.

— *It's clear that I can't hold a candle to Suzanne in the looks department. I'm so bland that I'm not surprised he prefers her.*

— *How come I don't have the backbone to stand up for myself and tell him how much his attitude is hurtful to me? Today, I could have fielded his left-handed compliment with something like, "Thanks for all of the other days in the past two years." I know this comes across as sarcastic and impolite, but at least this would show him I'm not a doormat and that I just let everyone walk over me.*

— *I've promised myself a million times to say no to him when he asks me to do everything for him, while Suzanne is either on the phone, filing her nails or pretending to work when he's around. Why can't I keep my promise? Jeez I'm dumb!*

Renee is beating herself up with rejection and allowing *Canta* to convince her this foolishness passes for the truth. Until she becomes aware of what she is truly experiencing, she will not be able to change her attitude. She is only looking at what is happening outside her orbit. In addition, she cannot even fathom that her boss is satisfied with her work, which is the reason why she is given the responsibility for things that are the most important. The fact he has not fired her is one more proof of his satisfaction that she doesn't even see.

The type of rejection she is experiencing with her boss reflects what she lived with her father or a male teacher regarding her school work or any other form of learning activity during her childhood or teenage years. Wounds of rejection and injustice can be traced back to the parent of the same sex. However, the parent (or someone else) of the opposite sex can activate these wounds if the parent of the same sex did not step in to help the child.

If Renee were to answer sarcastically and reactively to her boss, this would be attributable to her wound of betrayal. This would show her she doesn't understand why her boss, who has enough trust in her to give her important work to do, can't compliment her and show her his recognition.

> **Relationship wounds are linked to emotional relationships experienced in childhood. Professional wounds are related to all forms of learning.**

The fact that Renee does not turn against Suzanne can also be traced to her wound of rejection. She is unquestionably experiencing injustice with her colleague, but her wound of rejection is so significant that she has remained a conformist rigid person. If Renee loses control and blows up at her colleague, the wound of injustice will have trumped her wound of rejection.

If Renee were to decide to quit her job because she is fed up with her boss' attitude, it would be an indication that her wound of rejection has caused her to suffer to the point that she prefers to escape the situation rather than confront her pain. Like most who suffer, she is convinced that the situations and people are making her suffer. She simply cannot admit and even acknowledge that *Canta's* REACTION has completely taken over. As a result, she cannot be in contact with her great power to create her own life.

In conclusion, I hope you realize the importance of clearly detecting the wound that has been activated, since that is the only way you will be able to establish the link with an event from the past and move on to the next steps of the healing process explained in the following chapter.

Worsening the wounds

You have certainly noted by the increasing number of divorces, wars and especially major illnesses, be they physical or psychological, that our societies are plagued by increasing levels of suffering. Drugs and alcohol are the most widespread and easily accessible ways of deadening and concealing pain, and consumption continues to rise.

A neurologist recently told me that doctors feel over-whelmed by the many different types of dementia in the elderly. In cases where they cannot diagnose Alzheimer's or Parkinson's disease, they have lumped the many symptoms of brain cell degeneration under the heading of *Parkinsonism*. When I asked him how they treat this new disease, he replied they try out various things, without yet knowing what the results are.

Many of us have wondered why illnesses are on the rise at a time when science is very advanced. As far as I'm concerned, this is because we use medicine solely to treat ourselves and do not want to take responsibility for the attitude we feel in-side ourselves. That is a very important facet of our ego.

> **Since the ego does not want to recognize that we have the power to create our lives, it prefers to believe that problems come to us from the outside. It is systematically programmed to find a solution outside ourselves.**

It is common knowledge that pharmaceutical companies have taken great strides in creating numerous drugs that an-esthetize patients. People who go this route are not taking responsibility. They are merely deadening the problem and not facing up to it.

**As long as we do not take responsibility
for our problems, they keep coming
back stronger and in different forms.**

No doctor or drug can claim to heal you once and for all. We all know that if we undergo an operation or take a drug for the rest of our lives, the problems we are having will continue to manifest themselves.

The help provided by medicine or medication is certainly often required to relieve pain, but *ad hoc* use is preferable, if required. Any outside help, be it from general medicine, medication, personal therapy or any other help of your choosing, is far more effective if, at the same time, you accept that true healing can only be achieved within you. As soon as you're able to accept this, the healing process begins. The main goal of this book is to help you assume your responsibility.

**All physical disorders are merely
a reflection of the pain caused by
unhealed wounds of your soul.**

There is no doubt that if you have wounds causing great suffering, you must dig down inside yourself to find the necessary strength. You can tell a wound is significant by the pain you have been experiencing from a young age and by the fact you feel very powerless in coming up with a solution. You may also feel that you're suffering more than those close to you and especially that no one can help you. You can't see any light at the end of the tunnel.

I have mentioned several times that the wound of rejection causes the most suffering and that is why people are so much in denial about their suffering and don't want to feel it. Sadly, what they fail to realize is that the more they suppress what they are going through, the more the pain will return with a vengeance. With time, the pain will manifest itself in the form of obsessive fears and major health problems.

If you are struggling with a major and painful wound, this is an indication it has been developing over numerous lifetimes. During each life, your soul aspires to see it heal, but this cannot occur for as long as you allow your ego to manage your life. That is the major reason why the wound worsens with each life. If you wrap a bandage around an infected wound and do nothing else, it will get worse with time.

The more painful the wound, the more courage, strength, determination and perseverance is needed to confront it and regain control over your life. Making the decision is the most important step. After this, even though you may lack courage at times, if you really want to improve your quality of life, you will find some way to refocus yourself on your goal. Remembering where you want to go will be very helpful to your resuming contact with your inner power.

> ***Now that I have read this chapter, this is what I have decided to apply to my life:***

Now that I have read this chapter, this is what I have decided to apply to my life:

_____

_____

_____

_____

_____

_____

_____

_____

_____

_____

_____

_____

_____

_____

_____

_____

Chapter Nine

Healing and its benefits

You have no doubt realized while reading this book that the most important step in healing wounds is accepting them. It also means accepting the fact that your ego is convinced it is helping you by feeding you beliefs about each wound. Since it can only refer to what it remembers, it can't do anything else. It has no understanding of the needs of your soul, your being and your life plan.

As far as it's concerned, you could be reincarnated a hundred times, and it would still be relentless in its efforts to convince you to follow its line of reasoning. Don't forget that you did accept it initially. As soon as it realized that a new belief was helping to protect you, it soon resorted to this *modus operandi*.

Since the ego never dies because it is part of your mental makeup, you already had hundreds of beliefs when you were born. Everything you register during various lives both emotionally and mentally is etched into your soul which is immortal. You can compare the life of your soul to life on earth. Every day, you wear different clothes, spend time in different places, partake in activities and experience different emotions. Everything you live from day to day is consigned to memory.

Imagine, for example, that you engaged in a heated argument with a neighbour and went to bed that night racked by emotion, anger and uncertainty as to how to resolve the matter. The next day, the problem didn't solve itself just because some time went by. The wounds activated by this dispute are still causing you to suffer.

The incident may even seem more serious to you, if you had unconsciously ramped up your anger during the night. If you allow days or even months to go by, the unresolved problem causes you a great deal of hurt, not only emotionally and mentally, but also physically, which drains your energy.

On the other hand, if you reason that this neighbour doesn't get it and that there's no use trying to resolve this problem with him, that is known as *denial*. Every time you suppress a problem internally, it gets worse and causes you even more harm. Recall the previous example of a skin infection that you were wrapping up with a bandage so that you wouldn't see it.

The soul reincarnates for as long as it has not freed itself of these mental growths the ego feeds with unresolved problems. It carries all of the mental and emotional baggage accumulated during your numerous lives. Remember that growths are unnatural. Your body, a highly intelligent being, is always seeking to return to its natural state with the help of your inner GOD.

Try to imagine, for a moment, that your body is completely covered with large warts (physical growths). Could you feel comfortable with yourself and with others? I'm sure you'll answer no. You would go to tremendous lengths to get rid of these warts to feel good about yourself and with the people around you.

Your soul wants the same thing. It knows that being covered with mental growths (the ego's beliefs) is unnatural and that they prevent you from returning to true love, to peace of mind. That's why its automatic inclination is to reincarnate itself. Only in the material world can it free itself.

Healing and its benefits

After death, the soul realizes what has not been resolved and receives help from spiritual guides for its next life plan. Unfortunately, once the soul returns to Earth, it gradually starts forgetting, and during the first seven years of life, it begins to suffer, because the ego has been allowed to gain the upper hand. Why do we listen to our ego rather than the needs of our soul? Because it is crucial we begin to be aware just how much of a firm grip our ego has on us before we can manage to gain control of our life.

That is why my prime motivation is to come up with as many ways I can to help people become aware through the *Listen to Your Body* workshops, conferences and books. For example, participants in the workshop do many exercises among themselves to help them gain awareness more quickly, and they leave with actual methods they can put into practice during their daily lives. Remember that putting acquired knowledge into practice is very important.

> **Whatever work you do on your inner self, be it through books, conferences or workshops, nothing will change in your life until you adopt a new attitude and behaviour.**

My teachers and I regularly see people who ask the same questions from one workshop to the next. That's because they don't put into practice what we had suggested to them in the past and what would have helped them live different experiences.

This does not necessarily mean that everyone derives the same benefits. For example, after reading this book, you may quickly try out what has been suggested and the results will be beneficial. Someone else can go with the same suggestion and get different results. The difference between both will depend on how determined and willing you are to improve your quality of life.

There's only one way to find out whether or not advice benefits you, and that is through experimentation. Your judgment will then tell you which direction is best to take. Merely being open enough to take advice is an indicator that you really want to live some new experiences.

> **Openness to new experiences and new advice helps you remain in contact with your intuition.**

Even if the results are not as you had hoped, go with your heart to determine what the best choice is for you. Be attentive to the first answer that comes to mind. Intuition is always spontaneous. You must seize it when the opportunity presents itself. For the longest time, I wondered whether my ego or my heart was talking to me. The only way to tell is checking on how we feel. If we feel the slightest discomfort such as worry or fear, the answer is coming from our ego, not our intuition.

Let us take, as an example, the writing of this book, which is my twenty-fourth. I have experienced numerous situations where I was in my heart and others where I allowed my ego to take over. When I plan how a new book will be structured and I am feeling good, my mental energy is serving my heart to respond to the need of the moment.

However, when *Flyzy* gets involved, I begin to worry, I wonder whether I'll succeed, whether readers will like it, whether I'll have enough subject matter, whether it'll take too much of my time. As soon as I realize this, I must tell it this, even though it may take some time to do so: *Thanks very much, Flyzy. I know you worry about me, because you want me to be perfect and succeed. But I'd like to ask you to take a rest and allow me to organize this new book as I see fit. I really want you to trust me, as I feel able to take on any consequence that will come my way. I would ask that you don't do so in my place.*

You'll notice that I always suggest that you go with that last part each time you talk to your ego. The reason is that most of the time when we make a mistake or the results are not to our liking, we criticize ourselves. In reality, it's our ego criticizing.

Let's assume in the previous example that something un-expected comes up and I need twice as much time to complete the book, which has happened a few times. If that happens and I grumble the following: *Am I ever dumb! My customers will be disappointed, as they've been waiting for this book for two years. I shouldn't have allowed myself to be sidetracked. I should have been better organized. I shouldn't have gone on that extra trip, I shoulda, I shoulda... Yes, that's true, but it's not my fault. It seems to me I did my best... With my experience, I should have known that dealing with the unexpected is an in-creasingly more frequent occurrence.*

Ah, these little voices echoing in our head are a bother, aren't they? They never stop. Why is *Flyzy* still talking to me this way, even though I try not to think about it anymore? Because it is convinced it's at fault and that it should have warned me even more. It believes it's responsible for the consequences that befall me. It'll say: *I told you to pay attention to this or that. You'll see I was right, and now you're not happy. Listen to me next time!*

It'll continue talking to me this way until I have accepted it and shown appreciation for its efforts. So when I listen to my heart, I tell it: *Yes, Flyzy, I hear you and you're right. I know you wanted to help me with the concern you showed when I began the book and on several other occasions. Don't worry about me. True, I'm disappointed, but I promise it won't kill me, and that everything will sort itself out. There's certainly a good reason why the book came out later than planned. The future will tell. Thanks for being so concerned about me.*

As soon as *Flyzy* feels reassured that I'm not being accusatory, it fades away. Every time it does pull away, it is not boosted further and diminishes progressively, unbeknownst to it. Getting back to the example of the stain on the canvas that is not aware it's a stain, the same applies to *Flyzy*. It's not aware it's losing strength and influence over me. This is a gradual process that happens over years. At the same time the ego lessens, the influence of masks associated with wounds is also reduced.

Observing the wound instead of allowing the mask to lead

You're perhaps wondering whether you'll end up with no wounds one day. I don't know anyone who doesn't have any. I'm convinced it is normal and human to feel rejection, abandonment, humiliation, betrayal and injustice in life. When a wound is healed, it only means that your life is not dominated by what you are feeling. For example, you'll be aware that the comments someone says can make you feel rejection and be quickly able to see this in you, by saying that it is part of your human condition. The day you will love yourself and accept yourself unconditionally, you'll no longer feel that people are hurting you. Your perception of situations and people will have changed.

It is entirely possible that the following question has come to mind: *"In order for the masks to gradually disappear, can I manage to simply observe I've hurt myself without this pain causing me to suffer?"*

In Chapter four, I explained that true acceptance is the first step and the most important one in lessening the effect of wounds. Before accepting oneself, we must accept the good intentions of our ego and its virtual omnipresence in our lives. We must especially admit that WE are the ones giving it the entire floor.

Acceptance is only possible if we shoulder our responsibility. As is the case in all my books, I am repeating the definition of responsibility here. I believe it bears repeating, because the ego rejects this spiritual notion. Only after reading it or hearing about it numerous times do we manage to truly integrate it.

> **Being responsible is recognizing that we constantly create our lives and that we must assume all of the consequences of our decisions, actions and reactions.**

It is also recognizing that the same applies to those close to us, which means we are not responsible for their decisions.

You are responsible when you agree to follow the three steps mentioned in the preceding chapter to help you discover which wound has been activated. You then become aware that your perception and the reaction of your ego is creating the pain, not the situation or the person. You accept the idea that the fear your ego feels for you affects your perception of and reaction to a situation.

In summary, this is what is happening for all of us:

— A wound is activated and we experience pain;

— In a split second, on goes the *mask*, with the belief we will suffer less;

— Our ego doesn't know that the reactive behaviours of the *mask* create a lot of discomfort in and around ourselves;

— To trigger the healing process, we must come to the realization, as fast as we can, that we are no longer ourselves.

— We are then able to observe the activated wound, knowing it is normal and human to have wounds;

— The next step is a discussion with *Canta* to thank our ego for wanting to help us and to reassure it that we are now setting out to be what we want to be;

— That's when we stop all reactive behaviours, and our heart is once again at peace.

You have to go through the steps of acceptance and taking responsibilities in order to reach this stage of observation. It will then be easier for you to speak to *Canta*, and that will be proof you are able to clearly observe your wound. I remind you that each time you read the name *Canta*, it is preferable that you replace it with the name you have given to your ego.

You have been able to see from what you have read that our ego often runs our life and that we are constantly switching masks. However, not all wounds are activated to the same extent.

The greater the accusation and judgment, the greater the pain and fears.

When a situation or someone causes you to react a great deal and you want to be in a position to observe the wound and not suffer, you will have to truly forgive, which will be explained in this chapter.

Several of the examples given previously do not deal with acute pain that hurt for years and years, i.e. don't need forgiveness. Let us revisit some of these examples, starting with criticisms of others.

— *Did you see how big she has gotten? Does she not have a mirror at home? (I would never let MYSELF get that way. I have more willpower than she does).*

— *He never stops talking. He just takes over the floor. Doesn't he realize that the others would also like to talk? (I am more discreet and attentive to other people's needs).*

— *What's that fool doing on the road? He cut me off and almost plowed into me. How come he has a driver's licence? (I drive a lot better than that – I'd never do that).*

— *Poor thing, it's one problem after another, and she is becoming more and more of a victim. (I take charge of my life, I don't seek attention through MY problems. I don't take advantage of other people like she does).*

— *I'm fed up always having to repeat things. Seems to me what I'm saying is clear! (I listen better, I'm more attentive and quick to catch on to everything).*

If you see yourself reacting this way, it's an indication you are controlling yourself not to be like those you're criticizing. If ever you acted like these people, you'd criticize yourself and would not be accepting.

Here are some criticisms that others have aimed at you:

— *That new dish is rather tasteless. (It figures. I'M a lousy cook.)*

— *My friend's mom is not always criticizing him. (I'M a bad mother). My friend's dad takes time out to play with him. (I'M a bad father).*

— *That's the third time you've made the same mistake. How long will it take for you to get it through your head? (I'M a dummy, not worth a damn).*

And now we'll finish with a few examples of self-criticism:

— *I lost my cool again with the kids. When am I finally going to learn to be more tolerant?*

— *I really didn't need that second piece of cake. When will I have more will power?*

— *I hope MY husband will not notice that I haven't had time to put everything away. I'm so disorganized.*

— *How come I'm not as pretty as my sister? It's not fair.*

In all of the situations described earlier, if the comment or accusation does not last long, or if you forget about it quite easily, it means your wound was only slightly activated. Then you can talk to *Canta* this way: *There you go again Canta, still trying to help me in your own way. I know your intention is for me to be perfect in everything. I know as well you want to avoid having me suffer, if I don't reach that level of perfection. NOW I'm willing to assume any consequences that come my way, even if I'm not that perfect. I want to experience allowing myself to be a human with strengths and weaknesses. But thanks for your help. I'm giving you time off. You can go rest and watch me make my decisions alone from now on.*

While practicing this new approach for a few weeks, you'll see that Canta will become increasingly more receptive and will not come back quite as often on the same subject. His involvement will not last as long either.

The most important thing in your conversations with Canta is that it MUST FEEL YOU ACCEPT IT, EVEN THOUGH IT OFTEN SCARES YOU AND IS NOT AWARE OF YOUR TRUE NEEDS. It must especially feel that you truly appreciate its good intentions.

The additional steps of forgiveness

In situations that you have encountered repeatedly with someone, if your anger gets bigger every time and the pain you feel is more intense and lasts longer, this is an indication that the situation and the person in question are profoundly affecting a wound. You'll have to go through further steps to put yourself in position to observe the wound. These are the steps of true forgiveness.

Most of my books, workshops and conferences touch on this issue, because forgiveness is essential in order to completely reverse a situation. Its positive effects are miraculous. At *Listen to Your Body*, we had a chance to hear thousands of personal accounts and were able to see for ourselves the physical, emotional and mental effects of forgiveness. That is why I am always pleased to repeat the seven steps of forgiveness that are an integral part of our teaching.

Become aware of emotions and accusations

This step is described in Chapter eight and explains which wound has been activated.

Take responsibility

This step is achieved when you discover that the fear residing within is being fuelled by your ego and when you realize and admit that this fear is distorting reality. This fear is also why you had expectations of the person in the situation in question.

Being responsible is admitting that no one in this world is in your life to meet your expectations which stem from a lack of love of yourself. The responsibility step may take some time, but please don't give up – your heart wants to get there. The more serious the wound, the greater the grip your ego has, and the more effort you'll need to see the situation with the eyes of your heart.

Reconciling with the other person

Now that you have felt the fear inside you and recognized your expectations, reconciliation – the next step – will be easier. Seeing the other person as your mirror image is a great way to achieve this. You are probably already familiar with this method that we have been teaching for more than 30 years now, but I feel obliged to repeat it as often as I can.

I have often seen people who were convinced they were going about this method the right way, only to discover several years later that they had misinterpreted some steps. Their ego was clearly getting in the way, terribly fearful of disappearing if they completed all of the suggested steps.

In order to give you a better grasp of the mirror method and make it part of your approach, let's look at one of the examples we cited earlier:

— *I'm fed up always having to repeat things. Seems to me what I'm saying is clear! (I listen better, I'm more attentive and quick to catch on to everything).*

Let's pretend that Mary is at her wits' end about having to repeat everything to her daughter Abby. Mary is convinced her daughter often lets on she has not heard anything or forgot, because she's reacting to her mother. Abby is doing this because she finds her mother is much more demanding with her than with her brother.

If Mary wants to cope with this type of situation without activating any wounds, she has to go through every one of the steps of the forgiveness process. In order to take the first step explained earlier, it is preferable that Mary sit down, relax, breathe calmly and take a drink of water. She then should ask herself how she feels, what she is accusing her daughter of with respect to who she IS, what she is afraid of for herself, and she should write down what comes to mind.

After making note of her answers and taking the time to come to grips with what is happening inside, Mary then moves on to the next step. She takes responsibility by accepting the fact that her emotions and her fear are brought on by the expectations she has of her daughter. Being responsible is admitting that her daughter is a reflection of what is in her, what belongs to her. If she looked in the mirror and saw that she had pimples, she'd know they are hers, not the mirror's.

Mary needs a mirror because her ego prevents her from seeing that she's sometimes like her daughter and that she doesn't accept it. The ego is convinced the only way not to suffer is to see the unacceptable states of being only in others, not in oneself.

The mirror method only works with accusations regarding the state of being and not what the other does. Let's assume that, in this example, Mary:

1. Is accusing her daughter of being *unfair, selfish and ungrateful, no matter what she tries.*

2. Feels *rejected, unappreciated and unloved.*

3. Fears *being judged a bad mother, a meanie; and*

4. Acknowledges that she is expecting very much that her daughter prove her love for her.

Only when Mary assumes her responsibility will she know that Abby is accusing her mother of the same things, feels the same way and has the same fear for herself in this situation. She will realize that her daughter also has expectations and that she is reacting, because her expectations have not been met.

To be successful at reconciliation, the third step, Mary must put herself in her daughter's shoes and get a good feel for what she is experiencing. By opening up her heart, she will have a great deal of compassion for Abby. She'll then write: *I know now that Abby accuses me of being unfair, selfish and*

ungrateful for everything she does for me. She also feels re-
jected, unappreciated and unloved like I do. Her expectations
are not being met either, because she's afraid of being labeled
a bad and mean daughter.

I must point out that this mirror method is very subtle and
that you must be very attentive to the traps your ego sets for
you, as it wants to turn away the mirror. When someone makes
a remark or criticizes you, whether constructive or not, you
mustn't tell them you are their mirror and that they should see
themselves through you. This exercise is to be done by YOU
only. This person is passing through your life so that YOU see
yourself through them, not the opposite. Your ego wants the
other person to take themselves in hand, rather than see what
you experience when criticism is directed your way.

Self-forgiveness

This is the most important step and the one that guarantees
that you will never relive this kind of situation with this person
the same way. This step is so miraculous that if the unsettling
situation were to recur, we would describe it differently and
experience it differently without any pain. The reason is that
we have managed to see this through our heart, not through
our ego and our wound.

To get to this point, Mary must simply give herself the right
to be upset with her daughter, while acknowledging that this
was caused by her fear and her unfulfilled expectations. She
must also admit that since her wounds have not healed, she
sometimes is like Abby whom she has accused so many times.
In this example, the wounds of rejection and injustice were
active in Mary and Abby. As a result, they donned their *with-*
drawer and *rigid* masks.

Mary accepts the fact she is human, that she has wounds that are readily activated. She admits she is seeking the love of her daughter, because she doesn't love herself enough. The more she learns to love herself and accept that she is not always a good mother according to her daughter's expectations, the fewer expectations she will have of her daughter.

Self-acceptance, though, is not necessarily easy. The main reason is that when we assume our responsibility, this can open our wound of rejection. *Canta* could whisper the following in Mary's ear: *You're not a good mom. Here you've been accusing her all this time when, in fact, you're just like her. Abby really has good reasons to reject you. Why haven't you realized that she is there to reflect how you are? You're so dumb. What a poor mother you are!* If Mary keeps wearing her *withdrawer* mask, she'll feel increasingly worse. She won't be able to make her way through all of the steps and talk to her daughter. Her ego, which has been given a boost, will find other good reasons to sidetrack her from the process.

It's important that Mary recognize her humanity, her wounds, her fears and that she give herself the time she needs to get through this step and all of the others. She will gradually feel compassion for the little girl within who is suffering out of fear of not being loved. When she comes to realize she had been saddled with this fear for years, she will not have to give any excuses for acting this way with Abby. She will know down deep that she couldn't have done any different, as she was not even aware of this fear she had.

Connecting with a parent

This step will help Mary feel even more intensely the suffering of the little girl in her and check the extent of acceptance following the preceding step. (The link must be established with the parent who gave rise to the wound and is of the same sex as the person we are having a hard time with.)

In Mary's case, she can therefore deduce that the disagreement with her daughter reactivates the wounds of rejection and injustice traced back to her mother. When she is able to feel just how fearful she was of being rejected and not loved by her own mother, her heart will open more. She will know that she and her mother have lived and are still living with the same suffering she is enduring with her daughter. You can see this is one more illustration of the *triangle of life* which has come up several times in this book.

It is highly likely that her mother experienced the same pain with her grandmother. Until such time that this has not been truly forgiven, in other words, until there has been unconditional acceptance, the same problem will be passed on from one generation to the next, since it is triggered by unhealed wounds. The same accusations, the same feeling, the same fears and the same expectations are at play.

When Mary's heart opens slightly more from step to step, a feeling of liberation and immense gratitude will come over her, to the point she will be able to shed tears of joy in response to self-forgiveness which is so marvellous.

The desire to express what we discover

I strongly suggest that we express what we discover. This is the step where we can determine whether we've really forgiven ourselves.

In Mary's example, she visualizes herself sharing with her mother and daughter everything she has discovered about herself through the unpleasant situations she has lived with them.

Canta may dissent and tell her: *No way. Don't tell them all that. They won't understand. They don't know what true forgiveness is all about, and they probably won't want to listen to you anyway. They could even turn against you and tell you that you were at fault, not them. They will tell you they don't live this kind of fear and that it's your thing, that it has nothing to do with them.*

This type of resistance shows that Mary has not yet forgiven herself. Still scarred by her wound of rejection, she is still allowing her ego to influence her by wearing her *withdrawer* mask. Instead of accepting herself and recognizing her fears and her wounds, she is still mad at herself and continues to believe she is at fault, that she hurt her daughter and her mother, as was mentioned in step four.

In the workshops we offer at *Listen to Your Body*, we often observe that participants put up another type of resistance to the idea of expressing their discoveries. *Why must I see the person? Can't I do this in writing or over the phone?* In fact, when we have truly forgiven ourselves, our happiness is so great that we are anxious to share it with others.

As long as a form of resistance which generally indicates an underlying, unconscious fear persists, we can conclude that only partial forgiveness has been accomplished. Before we move onto the last step, it is important you ensure that all of the steps have been completed.

I repeat it is only normal and human to encounter difficulties at certain steps. The most important thing is for you to love yourself enough to give yourself the time needed for each step. The decision to bring about true forgiveness is proof that significant progress has been made, and the hard part of getting there is that it is opposed to what the ego wants. That is the importance of finding out how you feel about the idea of sharing with the person concerned what you discovered within you because of this undesirable situation that has come up between both of you.

Seeing the person and expressing your position

Mary can elect to share what she has discovered and meet with her daughter and her mother at the same time or separately. She can tell them she has something very pleasant to share with them, a great lesson of life she has been taught thanks to them. By using what she discovered and resorting to the mirror technique to express herself, she can then speak of the link she has been able to establish between her daughter and her mother.

When you go through these steps, I suggest you check with the person to find out whether they have ever noted the same fear. If you feel they are receptive, you can keep them talking about what they felt and ask them whether they judged you the same way you did them and whether they felt the same as you did.

When the other person doesn't want to speak to you about their feelings, don't insist. What you are sharing is an important step FOR YOU alone. It is the final step in the process to help you find out down deep inside whether you have forgiven yourself. If the other person refuses to speak to you or they react trying to defend or justify themselves, that is an indication that you have not forgiven yourself yet. So do not insist and please give yourself more time to do it before speaking to the person again.

There's no doubt we are happy to think that someone can learn something at the same time as us and that this exchange helps them be at peace with themselves. However, this must not be the goal of our exchange. When the person doesn't want to share, they are often too emotional or too awkward in expressing themselves. We mustn't come into this with expectations. They will go about forgiving themselves gradually, whether consciously or not. Like you, they have the right to take the time they need to get there.

The benefits of true forgiveness

One of the benefits of self-forgiveness is the significant improvement in our relationship with the person in question. We discover them from another angle We can see numerous qualities in them that escaped us because of the accusations we levelled at them, and we no longer feel ill at ease at the idea of seeing the person and talking to them.

Another benefit is that by not allowing your ego to trump your heart, you will regain your natural energy that was thwarted every time you donned a mask. Since this energy could not circulate, you had to dip into your energy reserve. When you manage your life yourself, you will discover the happiness that comes with using your energy to manifest your desires and your needs.

In our example with Mary, she had to be courageous and humble to forgive her mother and daughter, but the reward is such she will feel like doing this again at other times. She has applied a balm to her wounds of rejection and injustice, which has helped reduce their effect.

The same applies to each one of us when we listen to our needs. Every small or major decision made with our heart will diminish our wounds. Every act of love to ourselves will boost our energy and lift a weight off our shoulders.

Personally, I like to depict the beliefs I allow *Flyzy* to drag around as weights in the form of small and large rocks in a bag that I am lugging behind me, chained around my body. Some also say that we are chained and imprisoned by all of our fears and beliefs.

Now that you'll be increasingly able to confront your fears by accepting their presence without allowing them to manage your life, just imagine yourself emptying the rocks from your bag. You'll lose increasingly less energy dragging them around, and you'll be able to use the energy you gain to love yourself and meet your needs.

The benefits of gradually healing wounds

Physical changes

As your wounds diminish, you will notice physical changes. This comes on very quickly for certain people. I myself have witnessed such changes over the course of a two-day workshop. One person lost a few centimetres on his waist, another stood straighter and another one regained his natural voice that replaced the low voice of a *withdrawer*, etc.

For most people though, changes take place gradually. Here are a few examples of clients who have shared the great transformations that materialized after a year or more of work on them.

— Several men lost volume in their shoulders and belly, which gave their bodies better balance, as did the women in their hips or upper thighs (wound of betrayal).

— Some women saw their feet get longer by one or two shoe sizes. They felt more connected to the earth (wound of rejection).

— Some women had firmer breasts or buttocks (wound of abandonment).

— Some men had a larger penis (wound of rejection).

— Some had more flexibility in their joints (wound of injustice).

— Others stood straighter (wound of abandonment).

Here are some changes I have experienced personally in the last several years.

— Before, I needed to wear clothes one size larger for the lower body (wound of betrayal), whereas now, my upper and lower body are the same size.

— One of my breasts was far smaller than the other (wound of rejection), and now they are equal in size.

— My hair has much more body and is thicker (wound of abandonment).

— My bones got bigger, not smaller (wound of rejection) as is ordinarily the case for seniors.

— The contraction of the wound of rejection in my upper chest has disappeared.

— The arthritis that was starting to deform my fingers cleared up. (wound of injustice)

However, do remember that it is important not to have any expectations regarding physical changes. There is no "trick" involved. These changes take place on their own, and you must trust your body to have the ability to regain its natural state by itself. The important thing is that you feel increasingly better in your body. It's how you feel that indicates whether you have reduced your wounds, not necessarily physical changes. I have noticed that people who are more naturally physical seem to have more apparent changes than other people do. Those who are less physical notice changes that are less visible, for example, the digestive system, the heart, the lungs, etc.

Interrelated wounds

I have learned over the years that we very often resort to actions to lessen our wounds of betrayal and injustice which are the most apparent. Consequently, the wounds of abandonment and rejection diminish at the same time, since they are always present behind the other two.

Most elderly persons become softer and smaller over the years because they have not given enough recognition and accepted their wounds of abandonment and rejection. They resurface, and with age, become more apparent than the wounds of betrayal and injustice. That, in itself, is an excellent motivation to love ourselves and get back to being ourselves throughout our lives. We can then continue to have an active life as we age.

The disappearance of wounds

I am often asked how long it takes to rid ourselves of all wounds or what a body without wounds looks like. For as long as we are alive, we live with emotions and fears associated with our wounds. However, all of us must make it a point not to have them run our lives.

Let's assume you have a very straight and firm body that reflects a wound of injustice. If you do little or no work on yourself, your body, as it ages, will suffer disorders and illnesses attributable to your rigidity such as arthritis or stiffness in your knees or legs. Your joints will become more ankylotic, and you risk being constipated. If, on the other hand, you do various things to help yourself wear the *rigid* mask less often, you'll be pleased to note that the aforementioned problems will not surface or will disappear, if you were already suffering from them.

You'll probably continue maintaining your upright and firm posture, which is part of a rigid person's nature. However, you will no longer display the abnormal rigidity that is noted in someone who is overly rigid and narrow-minded.

The same principle applies to all wounds. For example, someone who is overweight due to a wound of humiliation shall remain round in spite of the work they have done on this particular wound, though they still feel good about themselves and encounter no physical problems caused by their excess weight. It is also worth pointing out that "normal weight" charts were originally developed by insurance companies.

> **What we consider *normal* was
> established by humans. It is not
> necessarily *natural* for everyone.**

Round or portly persons can be very agile, have boundless energy and lead a life that effectively responds to their needs. They allow themselves to be sensual and wear attractive clothing that suits them. They don't try to appear thinner or lie to themselves, but they choose colours rather than wearing just black and adapted clothing, nothing that is too small.

Abating fears associated with wounds

It is certain that each act of love that attenuates a wound brings about rather significant changes in how we think and act. Our family members often spot it before we do. Personally speaking, my children and clients I occasionally encounter during my workshops bring it to my attention. For example, I was told that I had become gentler with participants when, in fact, I hadn't even realized my attitude toward them had changed. Remarks like that are little rays of sunshine in our lives and confirm that gradual transformations can and do take place.

Once again, it is important that you don't have expectations, as this would indicate control. By accepting all facets of your humanity, especially your vulnerability, as often as possible, you will note that the results will naturally take care of themselves.

Your behaviour and attitude will improve when the main fears associated with each wound diminish. The following is a reminder of these fears with an additional explanation.

The fear of panic by the withdrawer (rejection)

This fear comes over you when you believe you're dumb and worthless. When you're at that point, you feel you're in a black hole, that there's no solution and that you'll disappear for good, in other words, cease to exist. *Canta's* first reaction is to convince you to flee. The number of ways is endless—wander in astral (absent minded) and freeze on the spot, run away, take drugs, sleep, work, and the list goes on and on.

It is only normal for you to have trouble admitting to this fear which has probably been very carefully concealed until now. It's impossible to see it or feel it, if you flee as soon as you panic. You then never have the time to feel the acute fear that comes with panicking.

> **The more a fear is hidden, the more it grows in scope to the point that the person has been pushed to their limit.**

By healing your wound of rejection, instead of allowing your fear to invade and control you, you will be increasingly able to get through the following steps more quickly, which will bring you closer to your **great need of allowing yourself the right to exist**.

— Start by taking several deep breaths, and drink some water if you can.

— Pay attention to the fear lurking inside you, and you'll know it isn't real—it is merely imaginary. *Canta* is the one encouraging you to react, believing that it is helping you by not having you feel the pain of your wound.

— Thank your ego for wanting to protect you. You'll add that you now know that this fear is preventing you from responding to an important need in your life and that you feel ready to face any consequences that may come your way.

— You'll take action to move in the direction of your need, and it'll be a good indicator of the love you have for yourself. It bears repeating—only the love you give yourself over and over can diminish your wounds.

The dependent's fear of solitude (abandonment)

You experience this fear when you're convinced that you're not loved and you feel immense sadness and anguish at the idea of ending up alone. *Canta's* first reaction is to get you to do some fancy foot-stepping, ignore your needs and put up with anything from loved ones, even be sick if you have to gain attention or scrap your projects if you are not supported by someone else.

It is highly likely that you won't feel this fear if you go out a lot, spend hours on the telephone or fulfill your need for a presence by watching television as soon as you're alone. You can even maintain relationships that you don't care for just to avoid that feeling of solitude. There is every chance that the controlling side of you will act independently to convince yourself that all is fine when you're alone and that you don't need anyone else.

By healing your wound of abandonment, instead of allowing your fear to overcome and control you, you will be able to go through the aforementioned steps increasingly quickly.

This will lead you to fill a **huge need, i.e., recognizing your strength**.

The masochist's fear of freedom (humiliation)

You feel this fear when you desire or dare allow yourself the freedom of fully enjoying sensual pleasures. You are then ashamed of your desires and actions, and you feel everyone is judging you, especially God. *Canta's* first reaction is to encourage you to listen to others' needs and tend to them relentlessly, ignore your own needs and take on other people's responsibilities, thereby curtailing your freedom.

It is highly likely that you don't even feel this fear, because you have convinced yourself you are always free to help others, and that it's up to you to choose. You delude yourself just as often into thinking that you're doing so out of pleasure, without first determining whether that is really the case. Your loved ones can see it more easily than you that you are rarely free to heed your own desires because of all of the obligations you take on.

By healing your wound of humiliation, instead of allowing your fear overcome you and control you, you will be able to go through the steps mentioned previously (for the fear of the *withdrawer*) more quickly.

This will lead you to fill your **great need of allowing yourself to be sensual.**

The controller's fear of dissociation (betrayal)

You experience this fear when there is a risk of a separation or breakup of some kind, which can be either a short or a long-term event. You believe that a strong person doesn't have the right to let go of something or someone. You believe you're familiar with the needs of persons of the opposite sex and if they don't go along with you, it's a sign they don't love you, which could result in a separation. So then, you fear losing control, being judged as weak and losing the trust others have in you.

In this case, *Canta's* first reaction is to encourage you to do everything you can to gain control over the other person and to lie, if possible, or accuse them to protect yourself. Your ego will convince you you're entitled to be impatient, bossy and skeptical, since they're the one causing you pain. It says you must absolutely give them the impression you fear nothing or no one and that you're reliable.

It is highly likely that you're not even aware this fear resides within you. By being bossy and controlling, you're convinced the others are the ones behind the quarrelling and disputes and they are steering you toward a separation.

In the case of a long-term separation, it is not uncommon for someone to manipulate the other person to get them to take the initiative to avoid feeling the fear of separation when, in fact, you were the one who wanted the separation in the first place.

By healing your wound of betrayal, instead of allowing your fear overcome you and control you, you will be able to go through the aforementioned steps for the fear of the *withdrawer* more quickly.

This will lead you to address a **huge need, i.e., allowing yourself to be vulnerable.**

The rigid person's fear of coldness (injustice)

You sense this fear when you feel you are being criticized or when you are faulted by someone of the same sex as you or by yourself. *Canta's* first reaction is to tell you you are imperfect, you reacted badly, you should have done this or not done that, etc. Your ego then helps you find excuses that justify your behaviour, and then makes you promise not to act like that ever again. You must do everything you can to appear perfect and nice in other people's eyes. You must especially hide your feelings.

As a rigid person, you probably have trouble recognizing that you're afraid of coldness, because you consider yourself warm, likable and nice. Moreover, since your self control is good and you're able to conceal your anger well, you don't believe other people could ever think you're cold. You don't realize that when you smile or claim that everything is good, your eyes and body betray you.

Another way of verifying the extent to which you are afraid of appearing cold and inattentive to others is noticing the number of times you are upset with yourself for not having been nice or kind-hearted enough with them and you're afraid of how they will judge you.

By healing your wound of injustice, instead of allowing your fear overcome you and control you, you will be able to go through the steps (for the fear of the *withdrawer*), more quickly.

This will lead you to fill your **great need of showing your sensitivity and allowing yourself to have limits.**

I will conclude the description of the major fears of each wound by reminding you of the triangle theory which holds that your fear of being a certain way with others is equal to the fear that others have in dealing with you and how you feel about yourself. The day you are able to recognize this and see yourself experience the same fear on all three sides, you will know it is significantly decreasing.

Returning to your natural state

As the wounds diminish, you will be pleasantly surprised to discover that you will gradually return to a natural state of being and will no longer take on the personality traits of the various masks. Your strengths and talents previously repressed by your fears will be able to resurface.

During our lives, all of us assume various personalities to be loved, to meet the expectations of other people and those close to us out of our fear of being wounded. As a result, we have lost our individuality, in other words, what we truly are, including our strengths and weaknesses.

For this very reason, you will experience the happiness that comes with getting back to the person you really are by accepting who you are at all times.

> When our heart guides us, we stop criticizing. We take advantage of every experience to learn to love even more.

The following pleasures await as you strip your ego of its power to run your life.

REJECTION: instead of taking on the personality of a *withdrawer*, you will discover you are quite able to be **effective**. No longer will you want to escape, hesitate to take your rightful place or consider yourself dumb or worthless. You will adopt new behaviours and attitudes that will be more natural for you.

— With your new-found levels of high endurance, you will be able to work as much as you want without feeling any stress.

— Your natural ability to create, invent and imagine will develop.

- You will still be a perfectionist but not an idealist. Instead of becoming obsessed with a task and revising it several times, you will settle for doing it only once. You'll be able to feel good, even if you have made a mistake or forgotten a detail.

- You will know especially that **you are not what you do**. When you make a mistake, you won't automatically conclude that you're dumb.

- The same applies when someone else will criticize or ignore you. A feeling of rejection will come over you for a moment, but it will quickly dawn on you that the criticism relates to what you've done, not to who you are.

- You'll have the pleasure of discovering the world as it really is, because you'll be more present.

- When you have to explain something, no longer will you feel obligated to provide a lot of details or repeat yourself several times to make sure the other person is not rejecting your idea.

- Your natural talent of being able to confront an emergency will be put to better use, since your fear of panicking will have been reduced.

- You will be increasingly able to complement yourself, instead of having to think only about your weaknesses.

ABANDONMENT: instead of adopting the personality of a *dependent* person, you'll be able to put your tremendous ability to be ***autonomous*** to use. No longer will you count on the love of other people to prove that you are lovable. You will take on new behaviours and attitudes that will come to you more naturally.

— You'll still be an expert when it comes to making requests, but this time, you'll do so without complaining or having any expectations. You will discover that even if the other person does not comply to them, it doesn't mean they don't love you.

— You'll remember to differentiate between *pleasing* and *loving* when it comes to other people.

— Consequently, you will not feel obligated to please everyone to prove to them that you love them. You will therefore be able to say *no* without being afraid of losing their love. When you say *yes*, it will be because you are willing, which will mean you do not have any expectations.

— You'll no longer put your talents as a comedian to use merely to gain attention. You'll know when the time is right to do so.

— When you relate facts to people, you will gradually be able to simplify and synthesize what you have to say, instead of launching into long-winded explanations just to keep the spotlight on you a bit longer.

— You'll be increasingly able to make decisions alone, without anyone else's agreement or support.

— When loved ones disagree with your projects, you will know they are entitled to have a different opinion or not want the same things as you do. You'll remember especially that they'll love you, even though they do disagree.

— You will make use of your great artistic talents just for your pleasure, not to attract attention.

— You'll always prefer being in the presence of others, but you'll also be able to be comfortable, even if you're alone.

HUMILIATION: instead of adopting a *masochistic* personality, you'll be able to put to use your tremendous ability to be *sensual*. You'll no longer strive to curb your sensuality, and you will take on new behaviours and attitudes that will come to you more naturally. You'll allow yourself to listen more to your needs and have a natural ability to recognize what they are.

— You'll always be able to be accommodating; however, you'll be able to determine when the time is right for you to help or not help others.

— You'll be better able to respect other people's freedom by discarding the idea that you have to resolve their problems. You'll take the time to determine whether they want any help before you act.

— Whenever someone asks you for help, you'll consider your needs before saying *yes*. You'll know that you don't always have to tend to others and thereby deprive yourself of personal freedom.

— Your newly acquired freedom will entitle you to enjoy each of your senses in all spheres of your life.

— You will allow yourself to show your highly jovial side that is striving to express itself. It will help to take the drama out of some situations and get a laugh from others, which everyone around you will really enjoy.

- You'll be able to accept the roundness of your body, and you'll gradually get to a suitable weight, even though it isn't necessarily considered *normal*.

- You will allow yourself to enjoy a fulfilling love and sexual relationship without feeling any guilt.

- You will feel increasingly worthy of what you are and be proud to be what you are.

BETRAYAL: instead of adopting the personality of the *controller*, you'll be able to put to use your tremendous ability to be a good **leader**. No longer will you have to prove your strength to have control over your environment. You will take on more natural behaviours and attitudes.

- You'll be a leader who doesn't impose their views and beliefs on others.

- Your public speaking skills will help others, not show your superiority.

- Your leadership skills and natural strengths will set an example for others to develop their own talents. It will then be easier for you to be in touch with their needs instead of wanting them to listen to yours.

- While maintaining your natural ability to make decisions quickly, you will also manage to take time to reflect on certain situations.

- You will experience less impatience and frustration when confronted by people who cannot do several things at once like you can.

— You will be able to surround yourself with people you can delegate work to. You will be more able to trust them and especially accept the way they perform a task, which may be as good or even better than your way.

— When you are in the presence of someone who is more talented than you are in a certain area, you will not take this to mean that you are weak. To the contrary, you will be glad to have the opportunity to learn something.

— You will be able to admit your faults or errors. You'll feel uncomfortable about lying and wanting to cause hardship for others.

— Your natural charm will make you likeable and you won't use it to seduce someone for the purpose of controlling them.

— You will allow yourself to be vulnerable and admit your fears or worries without thinking that you are cowardly.

INJUSTICE: instead of adopting a *rigid person's* personality, you'll be able to put to use your tremendous ability to be ***sensitive***. No longer will you have to want to please everyone or watch yourself to be perfect in the things you do and the way you appear. You will take on new behaviours and attitudes that will come to you more naturally.

— You will allow yourself to take breaks during your work, even though everything hasn't been done or is not perfect.

— Your quest for perfection will be useful in bringing beauty into your life, which is very important to you. You will not strive to do everything perfectly to be loved or appreciated.

- Details will always be important to you. However, you will remember that everything is but an experience and that perfection does not exist in the material world.

- Your ability to simplify complicated matters will be better balanced and will be a big help to you. Your explanations of various facts will not be too short, as you will know that not everyone has this talent.

- Your great natural sensitivity will increasingly show through, by allowing yourself to have a tear in your eye and even cry, or by being able to verify regularly how you feel.

- Your natural enthusiasm will be better balanced both personally and in dealings with others.

- Your physical appearance will always be important because of your quest for beauty and perfection, but you'll be comfortable, even if someone sees you without anything artificial.

As you can see, there are numerous and very apparent signs that point to the healing of wounds. This list of behaviours and attitudes that are more natural to you also serves as an excellent guide to provide you with goals you can reach.

In addition to everything that has just been mentioned, by being more present within and by allowing yourself to be what you are as much as you can, you will live more in the moment and be in contact with who YOU ARE. As a result, your sensitivity will be such that your intuition will be able to express itself the way it should. You will know much more quickly what you really need.

Knowing your wounds and masks better will also help you recognize the fears and needs of others. However, be careful not to fall into the trap your ego sets for you. It can easily get you to show others just how intuitive (clairvoyant) you are by impressing them, controlling them or being too directive with them. We put our intuition to good use when we help others discover their own needs, and the only way to do this is ask them the right questions.

As you accept your wounds, you will accept the wounds of those close to you. You will have compassion for them, which will avoid your criticizing them or judging them.

Conclusion

To complete this book, I suggest that you reread the last chapter of my book entitled *Heal your wounds and find your true self* where you will find other information that I have chosen not to repeat here.

All you have to do now is to keep putting into practice what you have decided to apply to your life, after reading each chapter. I remind you that learning something does not change anything in life. However, when we change our attitude and take different actions, it is at that point when change takes place. Until you have lived various experiences, you will not be able to discover what is best for you.

In conclusion, here is a complete definition of the term **healing wounds**.

You know you're on the path to healing when you're aware that a wound has been activated, that you are able to observe the pain caused by the wound and you allow yourself to be human.

You can verify that you have gone through
these steps when you do not feel the need
to wear the mask associated with the wound
and that you don't have any reaction.

Acceptance brings a sigh of relief,
gradually causes the pain to disappear
and brings you back to the present.

You then perceive the entire
situation as a lesson in life.

Now that I have read this chapter, this is what I have decided to apply to my life:

_____

_____

_____

_____

_____

_____

_____

_____

_____

_____

_____

_____

If you would like to be notified when Lise Bourbeau's next book is released, send us your contact information...

... by e-mail: info@leseditionsetc.com

... by fax: 450-431-0991

... by mail:

Les Éditions ETC
1102 Boul. La Salette
St-Jérôme (Québec)
J5L 2J7 CANADA

The BE yourself workshop

The dynamic and practical teachings of the BE YOURSELF workshop can help all those who really want to IMPROVE their quality of life. This one of a kind opportunity provides you with a solid foundation to pursue what you want out of life.

The workshop is divided into two different days* in Canada, and you can choose to participate in one or both sessions.

Day 1   **BE YOUR TRUE SELF**
         by letting go of what you believe you should be

Come find out what your current needs are and how to satisfy them in order to feel good and be happy. Step by step, you will discover a number of different tools, including the important step of discovering how much you really love yourself.

You will learn, among other things, how to...

♦ identify the fears and beliefs which serve as stumbling blocks to your happiness;

♦ discover what is preventing you from being who you want to be;

♦ deal with dissatisfaction and reach serenity;

♦ use the tools that are simple and necessary to be in harmony with yourself.

**Dare to take the first step and
come learn how to be yourself!**

Day 2   **BE YOURSELF WITH OTHERS**
            By improving your relationships with them

Come find out why your relationships and the situations you find yourself in are not always as you would like them to be. Then experiment and discover, step by step, what is possible so that you can establish healthy relationships and reach a state of well being with others.

You will learn, among other things...

♦ the real sense of responsibility, which will free you from feelings of guilt;

♦ the importance of making agreements, but also allowing yourself to change your mind.;

♦ to identify the source of the emotions that damage your relationships and how to deal with them;

♦ two proven methods to improve your relationships.

Use your difficult relationships as a springboard towards better well being!

For 30 years, thousands of people have decided to transform their lives with the help of our tools. You too can start today and be yourself!

Visit our website or call us
1-888-437-8382 or 450-431-5336
www.listentoyourbody.net

LISTEN TO YOUR BODY
Learn to be happy

C2

Find us on f

Join the **LISE BOURBEAU READERS CLUB**
and chat with members from
around the world.

We created a Facebook Group to bring together people from around the world who have a common interest in Lise Bourbeau's books and workshops.

Our primary intention is to offer YOU the opportunity to share your ideas, questions, and advice to other members of this group based on the Listen To Your Body philosophy, created by Lise Bourbeau.

Books from the same author

Listen to your best friend on Earth, your body

LISE BOURBEAU takes you by the hand and, step by step, leads you beyond "packing your own parachute", to taking that step back into the clear, refreshing stream of life that flows from the Universal Source. She gives you the tools, not only to fix what is wrong in your life, but to build a solid foundation for your inner house - a foundation that extends as far as the global village. In this book, she helps you build an intimate, rewarding and powerful relationship with the most important person in your life - yourself.

Your body's telling you: Love yourself!

Lise Bourbeau has compiled 20 years of research in the field of metaphysics and it's physical manifestations in the body and brought it all to the forefront in this user-friendly reference guide, Your body's telling you: Love yourself! Since 1982, she has worked successfully with over 15,000 people, helping them to unearth the underlying causes of specific illnesses and diseases. A comprehensive guide to the metaphysical causes of over 500 illnesses and diseases, is a succinct and visionary work that is truly and literally a labor of love.

Heal your wounds and find your true self

Do you sometimes feel that you are going around in circles in your personal growth? Do you occasionally see a problem re-emerge, thinking you had solved it? Perhaps it's because you're not looking in the right place.

This new book by Lise Bourbeau, as concrete as her others, demonstrates that all problems, whether physical, emotional or mental, stem from five important wounds: *rejection, abandonment, humiliation, betrayal* and *injustice*. This book contains detailed descriptions of these wounds and of the masks we've developed to hide them.

This book will allow you to set off on the path that leads to complete healing, the path that leads to your ultimate goal: your true self.

Books by the same author

Just listen to your body and eat - STOP trying to control your weight
Lise Bourbeau's new book has many goals:
... help you discover that there are six reasons besides hunger that make you want to eat; ... show you how much you control your food intake and how that can be bad for you; ... teach you to quickly recognize the emotional wounds that prevent you from eating well; and help you love and accept your body, and especially who you are at every moment.
This eagerly awaited book offers an entirely new way of looking at your relationship with your food. It reveals the connection between the physical, emotional, mental and spiritual dimensions of the person and can help you, in this

Cancer - A book of Hope
What would you say to having a different view of cancer, that notorious word that has scared — and continues to scare — millions of people every year throughout the world? Why not consider this illness, even with all its devastating effects, as a friend rather than an enemy that one must struggle against?
Cancer is not an inevitable fate but rather a message aimed at helping you recover happiness and inner peace. Cancer seen this way becomes an opportunity for transformation and for loving yourself.

EGO - The greatest obstacle to healing the 5 wounds.
With this book, the author really wants to help you discover the tremendous influence and power that your ego can have on you. You will learn to recognize the operating mechanisms of the five wounds and be better able determine when they are preventing you from simply being yourself, i.e. happy. By applying the techniques suggested, you will become aware of the countless occasions when your ego is controlling your thoughts, words and actions: a vital condition for healing and taking control of your life so that you can be your true self.

4 ways to order

TITLE	QTY.	TOTAL
	SUB-TOTAL	
	SHIPPING	
	TOTAL	

www.listentoyourbody.net

info@listentoyourbody.net

ECOUTE TON CORPS
1102 La Salette Blv
St-Jerome (Quebec)
J5L 2J7   CANADA

1-800-361-3834
or 450-431-5336

SHIPPING & HANDLING FEES
CANADA and US : 12$CAN
INTERNATIONAL: contact us

☐ VISA   Number: ☐☐☐☐☐☐☐☐☐☐☐☐☐☐☐☐   Exp.: ☐☐ / ☐
month   year

☐ MasterCard   Cardholder's name:_____

Signature: _____

☐ CANADIAN MONEY ORDER made out to ECOUTE TON CORPS

Name: _____

Address: _____

City/Town - State/Province:_____   Zip code:_____

Telephone #: (   ) _____   Country _____

C6